Other Titles by TW Brown

The DEAD Series:

DEAD: The Ugly Beginning
DEAD: Revelations
DEAD: Fortunes & Failures
DEAD: Winter
DEAD: Siege & Survival
DEAD: Confrontation
DEAD: Reborn
DEAD: Darkness Before Dawn
DEAD: Spring
DEAD: The Reclamation
DEAD: End

DEAD Snapshot – {your town here}

DEAD: Snapshot – Portland Oregon
DEAD: Snapshot – Leeds, England
DEAD: Snapshot – Liberty, South Carolina

Zomblog

Zomblog
Zomblog II
Zomblog: The Final Entry
Zomblog: Snoe
Zomblog: Snoe's War
Zomblog: Snoe's Journey

That Ghoul Ava

That Ghoul Ava: Her First Adventures
That Ghoul Ava & The Queen of the Zombies
That Ghoul Ava Kick Some Faerie A**
Next, on a very special That Ghoul Ava
That Ghoul Ava on the Lam
That Ghoul Ava on a Roll

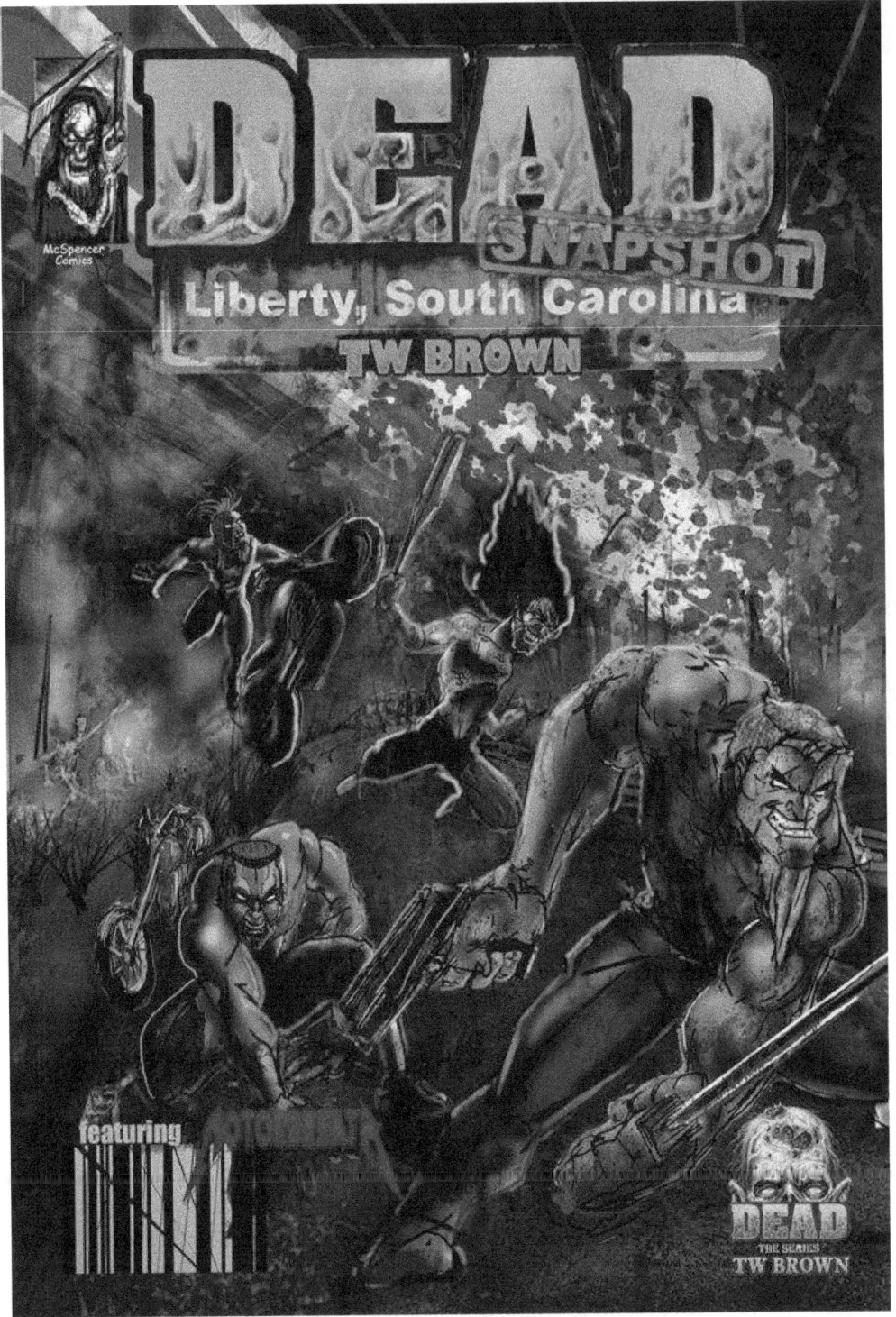

Available in paperback and ebook

TRIBUTE

TW Brown
Authortwbrown.com
Portland, Oregon, USA

TRIBUTE

I also want to thank Paul Brown Photography for his picture of Jason Fellman.

Printed in the U.S.A.

EAN—13: 978-1-940734-55-2

To everybody who dreams of taking
the stage

Author's Note

Every year, I try to write something that is outside of my genre. For those of you who are familiar with my zombie stuff…obviously this ain't it.

TRIBUTE hearkens to the days when I dreamed of being a journalist for magazines like *Circus*. Seriously, if you were an 80's metal fan, you have to be familiar with that magazine. My high school locker was wallpapered with pictures that I cut out from it.

This book came from my believing that there had to be something worth writing about when it came to the Portland, Oregon Tribute Band scene. The thing is, I really had no solid angle for the book as I went in. It wasn't until I started talking to many of the performers that I realized they all had some very solid advice about what it takes to be successful in the world of Tribute Band entertainment.

Advice is a funny thing. What works for one person might not work for another. That is why I set out to ask as many of these people as possible if they could give me what they believed to be a blueprint for success. Forgive me now for having that statement repeated throughout this book. I did try to re-phrase it a number of different ways, but it all boiled down to the same thing.

Besides those nuggets of advice, you will also get a peek behind the scenes. Not in a raunchy tabloid sort of way. Instead, I believe that you will meet a bunch of people that are just like you. The only difference is that their job is getting on stage in front of a crowd and singing, playing guitar, drums or keyboard, and putting on a show.

During this little journey, I gained an even deeper appreciation of the performers. I made some new friends, and I am even taking guitar lessons from the Slash character (Brandon Cook) from Appetite for Deception, the local Guns N' Roses Tribute Band. One of the biggest aspects that I took away from this experience is an appreciation for the level of hard work and business sense that it takes to be successful in this field. It is a lot more than just jumping up on stage and playing a few songs. These bands don't have teams of roadies and people to handle all their financial affairs. It is all done "in house" so to speak. That means these bands put in much more work off stage than on just to provide you with an hour or two of entertainment.

There were a few interviews that did not make it. That is not a reflection of the interviewees, it is simply a case of deadlines forcing me to make decisions. I appreciate every single person who gave me a few minutes of their day. I do wish I could have fit everybody in, but time has a way of moving past you when you aren't looking.

If you are picking this book up at *Harefest 6* where it is being debuted and have gone back to your spot in the grass, I hope that you like the photos that are included. With one exception, I took them all. I bet you will have no problem getting the subjects of those pictures to sign them. I know that is what I plan to do. I will also say right here that I am a writer, not a professional photographer. If my composition is funky or the main object is not centered just so…well, I refer you to the statement that I am a writer.

This book would not have happened if not for the wonderful men and women who gave me a bit of their time and submitted to my awkward style of interviewing. I could rattle of the list of names, but honestly, nobody wants to really read that. Hell, I imagine that a lot of you have skipped this entire introduction.

However, there is a few people that I owe a very specific thanks to. I will start with Don Evans. It was his band, Unchained, that first got me hooked. It was also thanks to his Facebook messaging that nabbed me a number of these interviews. Next is Mark Thomas. Mark turned me into an even bigger fan of Appetite for Deception with his open nature. He also opened up their rehearsal for me where I got to see just exactly why they are so damn good. Oh…and he and the Appetite gang will be appearing in an upcoming *That Ghoul Ava* adventure sort of like the classic *Scooby Doo* episodes that featured guests like the Harlem Globetrotters. So stay tuned for that.

Last, and by no means least, is Jason Fellman. I am not affiliated with or in the employ of J-Fell Presents. Let me make that clear. However, I probably would not have been able to write this book without his help. He was a constant and regular source of support throughout, and also acted as liaison between me and many of the artists. He really has shaped the landscape of the Tribute Band scene here in Portland. He is a business man and a musician. But above all that, he is simply one helluva guy.

TW Brown
June 2016

Contents

PICS

1

"Welcome to the show!"

"Hello, Portland, Oregon! Get on your feet, put your hands together, and please welcome...!"

The house lights dim and an ethereal mist from the fog machine begins to swirl about the stage. Dark figures move into position and the electronic crackle of a guitar pickup going hot cuts through the crowd that is already surging forward in anticipation. Men roar and women scream as arms extend to the rafters when a machinegun blast of drums shake the floor.

Guitars shriek and nimble fingers fly over the fretboard, unleashing more notes in a span of seconds than seems possible. The guttural thrum of a bass makes the feet tingle and the hairs on arms and necks stand on end.

The lights come on and wash the figures on the stage in hues of red, green, and purple. The lead singer wails over it all, long hair catching the light perfectly and absorbing that color and refracting a brilliant halo. The words are familiar and everybody in the crowd has no choice but to sing along to the familiar tune...for you, that one song is the entire reason you came, an anthem from a time in your life that you clutch tightly and revel in the thrill.

***

What you are about to read is a lot of observations and interviews that I gathered over a two-year period in Portland, Oregon. This is sort of the introduction and a summary of what you will find in the pages ahead.

If you are a fan of the Tribute Band scene, then you might already know a lot of this stuff. However, you might not truly realize just how accessible the performers you watch tend to be. Trust me, you don't need to be writing a book to have a conversation with these people. They are—believe it or not—just like you in many ways. The big difference is that they sing, play guitar or drums, and entertain.

Not one of the individuals that I spoke with considers him or herself a "Rock Star" in any way, shape, or form. They are just happy to be doing something that they love.

If you are a musician, and perhaps forming a Tribute Band is one of the things that you are mulling over in your mind, then I hope you might find a nugget of information in these pages that inspires you or points you in the right direction.

On any given weekend, there are multiple venues featuring live music. Portland, Oregon and the surrounding metro area are a hotbed for a scene that remains undiscovered by many. There are plenty of bands out there doing their own music, and that is great. I love seeing original acts…you never know if or when that local gem will be launched into the national spotlight.

And then, of course, there are those major recording artists that tour the world. Reunion tours…farewell tours…the seventh incarnation of the farewell tour (no, really, they mean it this time).

In the late 70's and through the 80's, I was a fixture in the concert scene. Groups ranging from KISS to Black Sabbath were now sharing the stages with everything from Dokken to W.A.S.P. As the 80's crept on, the stalwart heavy metal bands of the 70's were giving way to the upstarts like Quiet Riot and Motley Crüe. Some would burn hot and fast, while others remain (more or less intact) to this day.

The so-called "Hair Bands" were all the rage, and would make their way up the charts. They were loud, wild, and represented everything that parents hated and feared. Women wanted them, men wanted to be them. As trite as that might sound, it was true in ways unlike ever before.

Hair spray was burning a hole in the ozone…and we did not care in the least. Spandex, bandanas, and make-up were on the shopping lists of men and women alike.

I lived in that era, and I still love that music. Funny thing about music and the Generation Gap, everybody thinks that their era had it right. Toss in the whole thing about how "today's kids don't know what good music is" and you are preaching the same words that have been said since the days of Mozart and Salieri. We could spend the entire book talking about the differences in music over the ages.

However, this book is not about that. This book is about people you might have never heard of pretending to be people that you know and love. This is about the men and women who make up the Tribute Band scene.

Since I am living in and around the Portland, Oregon locale, I will be speaking about and sharing anecdotes regarding people from this specific region; however, if you do a little bit of searching, I bet you will find a thriving community of Tribute Bands in your area.

Honestly, I found mine quite by accident; and I didn't actually find it myself, my wife stumbled on a concert while trying to plan something fun for my birthday one year (but that is a story for another time). The first show we ever attended in the scene consisted of Cult, Van Halen, and Poison Tribute Bands. They played in a small venue that got its start as a Vaudeville theater at the end of that era and quickly converted to a cinema. It was a rather intimate setting for what would be a very entertaining show.

I had seen more than my share of cover bands over the years. Heck, I even played and sang in a couple. I was not really sure what to expect that night. I walked in thinking that this was basically a cover band with a focus. I would discover that was not exactly true.

The first thing you need to know is that a Tribute Band is not a cover band. Yes, they are covering material written by another artist, but a cover band will usually play music from a variety of artists. A Tribute Band sticks to one group. They might go as far as to dress up (including wigs if need be) in order to really capture the vibe of the band they are portraying.

There is a lot to be said for a band that is willing to take one artist and make it their goal to recreate the experience of seeing them in their heyday. Hell, Elvis impersonators have been doing it for years…so why not Van Halen?

Some bands are made for this type of venue; groups like KISS invite that sort of homage and, other than Elvis, they are perhaps the easiest to identify by sight. Seriously, how could you not notice a guy with six-inch-heeled dragon head boots and kabuki makeup?

However, the Tribute scene in Portland—which is arguably one of the best in the nation—sports everything from AC/DC to Zeppelin. (See what I did there with the whole A-to-Z thing?) Here in the Pacific Northwest, we even sport an outdoor music festival known as Harefest. (Harefest V took place during the summer of 2015 with a massive thirteen band lineup!)

So, before I start sharing some of the tales of these jukebox heroes, I want to share what got me hooked. It is a simple story really. As I said, it was my birthday, and the wife wanted to do something special. She knew that I am a big lover of my music. Seriously, I would take music over television any day of the week. She also knew the kinds of music I really love. Granted, I do have a varied taste—everything from classical to jazz to good old rock-n-roll. But I am partial to that 80's music scene that consisted of groups like Ratt, Mötley Crüe, Poison, and Van Halen. To be clear, I loved Sammy Hagar as Sammy Hagar, but I never really got into the Van Hagar thing. I was a Diamond Dave sort of guy.

I was treated to tickets to see a group called Unchained. The band is an all-out, balls-to-the-wall Van Halen Tribute Band. I honestly did not know what to expect. After all, I had seen the original thing back in their prime. My last Van Halen concert had been the *1984* tour, which I saw in San Diego, California from the third row on the floor.

When the band took the stage, I was right up front actually leaning on the stage; much closer than I had ever been to the real Van Halen. I seriously had to do a double-take when it came to the Eddie Van Halen impersonator. He had the look down to a science. This guy was EVH personified, even down to that trademark smile Eddie was so famous for flashing in all the classic Van Halen videos back in the day when Music Television was really MUSIC television.

The front man had a swagger and the attitude you loved about David Lee Roth without all of the vulgarity and propensity for forgetting the lyrics. He was jumping, spin-kicking, and doing flying splits off the drum riser. It was like stepping into a time machine and being treated to the best parts of a Van Halen show.

The bass player was not as frisky as Michael Anthony, but he had that presence. Also, his bass playing was spot on. Anybody who knows anything about music knows that the bass and drums are the heart of the engine. If those slip even a little, everything can spin out of control.

And the drummer? Well. While he never lit a gong on fire, he held court with the beats Alex laid down all those years ago.

It was after the show that really made for a special experience. The band came out to the crowd and mingled, posed for pictures, and thanked the audience in person. Can you imagine the real Van Halen doing such a thing? Maybe when they were a bar band…maybe.

That night, I got to actually meet the members and speak with them for the first time. I admit that it was more than just a little bit cool; in fact, it was almost like meeting the real deal. Seriously, they sounded great, dressed the part, and played almost all my favorite Van Halen songs with near perfection. I was even invited to pose with the band for pictures.

However, it was a few months later when I saw them play another venue that I became hooked. I was sitting with my wife in the restaurant part of the venue they would be performing at later in the evening when the band strolled in. Since three of the four wear wigs as part of their costume, you might not recognize them right away. However, they recognized us. In fact, Don Evans and Brad Halleck ("Diamond Donnie Lee" and "Shreddy Van Halleck" when they hit the stage) came over and said hello. Even more impressive, they remembered our names!

After some polite and pleasant conversation, they went to their table and ate or whatever it is that rock stars do before they hit the stage. However, this would be the start of my quest to really become an active fan of the Portland Tribute Band scene. Since then, I have been to well over fifty shows and seen some of the best (and even worst) performances in my many years as a live music buff.

Being somebody who is more than passingly familiar with the entertainment world, I will say that I expected a lot of one-upsmanship and even some backstabbing as I started circulating among these hard rock doppelgängers. Nothing could be farther from the truth. In fact, there was almost no bad talking about other bands during the months that I spent conducting interviews with many of the performers I will talk about in the pages to come.

There is a lot that could be said about this scene. It differs in many ways from the mostly undiscovered bands out there trying to draw crowds with their original music. Don't get me wrong, I love the local "original" music scene, but there is something almost comforting about hearing the music I grew up loving.

This is an ode and a celebration to the hard working individuals that take the stage and give their audience a chance to relive the music of their youth. For that span of time, it is like stepping into Mr. Peabody's "Way-Back Machine" and transporting to the apex of the careers of some of the most iconic bands of the 70's and 80's.

As I said, I saw most of the original versions of the bands I now watch on the Tribute scene back when they were in their prime. Heck, I even caught a few when they were openers for other artists and then again when they returned as the headliner. (Seeing Mötley Crüe open for Ozzy on his *Bark at the Moon* tour is one of the most amazing concert highlights of my youth.)

So what is it that I see in this music scene that can possibly fill up a book? Honestly, I could do a feature on most of the bands you will hear about. They all have amazing stories about why they do what they do. I could talk about the fans that are fiercely dedicated to these bands. There are many individuals in this area that don't miss a show, often attending concerts on back-to-back nights or at least catching several a month. What I will try to do is give you a taste of the whole thing. Also, I hope to share some tips if this is a road you are considering as a musician.

I was granted amazing access to a good number of these bands. Some were kind enough to chat with me backstage before going on, others had me in to their private rehearsal space, and some even paid a visit to my home to answer questions and discuss how they got into doing what they do. The hardest part for me was not turning into a total "fanboy" when meeting some of these guys.

The thing is, when most of these performers are not on stage, they are doing regular jobs just like the rest of us. There are dentists, insurance salesmen, construction workers, and a wide gamut of other "Regular Joe" jobs that these people do to pay the bills. Nobody is getting super rich playing in a Tribute

Band. They perform out of a love for it. Yes, there is a lot to be said about having a crowd of adoring fans, but one thing I think I feel safe saying is that these individuals are performing because they love playing music first and foremost.

Yes, they take their role seriously, but not to a point of being unapproachable. That brings to mind one moment that I will never forget at one of the first shows I attended. The band was Maiden Northwest—an Iron Maiden Tribute Band. There was a young man in the audience who was (and forgive me if I get this wrong) a guitar student of one of the band's guitarists. This young man is developmentally challenged, but he loves music and has the same guitar hero dreams that many young men have entertained at some time or another. During Maiden Northwest's set, they brought this young man up on stage. He plugged in his guitar and played the Iron Maiden song he had apparently been practicing.

To be clear, he was not "air guitaring" during his time on stage. I was in the front row and could see and hear him quite clearly. During his performance, the band made him one of their own. He headbanged with the bass player, strutted and posed with the vocalist, and riffed with the other guitarists. During his brief set, he was a full blown member of the band.

It is unlikely that you will see that sort of thing happening very often in any form of entertainment. Most performers are not willing to risk a moment of their performance time on such things; but that is just one thing that makes the Tribute Band scene shine bright.

Don't get me wrong, I don't have anything against the bands that these Tribute Bands portray. My issue is with how out of control prices have gotten when it comes to grabbing a few tickets for a night with your favorite band. Toss in the "special" add-ons that a person can purchase, and you are almost talking about having to take out a second mortgage.

Yes, the simple answer is that "if you don't like it, don't go, don't pay for the extras, et cetera." That is fine, but that only scratches the surface of my point. I guess the main thing I am trying to convey here is just how much bang you get for your buck when you catch some of the better Tribute Bands.

There are a lot of people that go to several of these shows a year. One of the big reasons is that they are amazingly affordable. Just to further illustrate my point, my daughter and I were in attendance for the real Mötley Crüe's farewell tour. We had very good seats on the floor for this event. With the price I paid for those two tickets, I could see at least two shows a month on the Tribute scene for an entire year. Don't get me wrong, I was totally stoked to see Vince, Nikki, Mick, and Tommy one last time, but I've seen Same Ol' Situation a few times (an amazing Mötley Crüe Tribute Band), and they bring it with authority. Plus, how can you complain about seeing over twenty-five shows for the price of one? Even if a couple fall flat, you still walk away on the plus side of the equation.

For the price (in most cases) of a movie ticket, you can often catch a double- or triple-bill of Tribute Bands. Imagine being able to see Ozzy, Metallica, and the Scorpions for less than twenty bucks! Okay, so you might not be seeing the actual bands, but some of these bands are not only just as good, but in many cases, better.

Better? Many of you might be skeptical about such a claim. I hate to break it to the diehard fans of some of the big bands like Van Halen, Def Leppard, and others, but it is very common for these bands to use backing tracks to cover their shortfalls. That is something you would *almost* never find on the Tribute scene. I have to say almost because I can't speak for every single act that hits the stage; I just know that would not go over well in the Portland scene.

Tribute Bands consist of musicians who work hard to sound as close to the real thing as possible. True, like any impression, nobody can be spot on, but it can be close enough that you would almost swear you are catching the real deal. One of the Portland bands that certainly gives the original act a run for the money is Portland's own Crazy Train. Tim Tugg will have you rubbing your eyes in disbelief that you are not seeing *the* Ozzy Osborne on that stage.

If you speak to him off stage, he is just a regular guy; however, once he adds the eyeliner and gets into character that includes the slightly slurred English accent and the slow shuffle across the stage, the resemblance is uncanny. I have even posted pictures from the show and had people begging to know where I found out about the new Ozzy tour.

Another bonus is that I have met some great people in the crowds while waiting for a show to start. Some have become friends that I have shared time with and spoken to away from the concert scene. We already know that we have at least one thing in common in our love for music; even better, we know we love the same kinds of music. We bond over being fans of Unchained, Stone in Love, Appetite for Deception, and so many others.

That is in contrast to when I go to an arena or other large venue to see a major act and am surrounded by thousands of strangers that I am not likely to interact with. I look forward to running into a few friends before a show and catching up on how they have been, or maybe meeting somebody that they have brought along to introduce to this amazing sub-culture.

One of the things I discovered quickly was that these guys are also fans of each other. It is not uncommon to see many of the familiar faces from the assorted Tribute Bands roaming about in the crowds during each other's shows. There is a support and camaraderie in this scene that I find lacking in many other aspects of the entertainment world. Also, many of these musicians play in more than one band and, as in any other relationship; it can be a mighty task to keep a lineup intact. You never know who you might turn to when a slot opens.

I hope that, as you read this book, you will come away with an interest in checking out your own local Tribute Band scene. Also, I hope that you might find it at least moderately entertaining as you learn about the real people behind the personas. Chances are, no matter where you are, you will find more of the same in your neck of the woods.

So come along and learn about the jukebox heroes that roll their sleeves up every day just like you. As I said earlier, most have regular jobs that they perform to keep the lights on and the groceries on the table, but, when the weekend arrives, they transform into something amazing and put themselves out there for the toughest critics in the world: fans of the actual bands they portray.

h blah blah .

2

Love at First Listen

You might be wondering right about now how this book could relate to you if you are not in the area surrounding Portland, Oregon where I took in these shows and met the members of all these amazing bands. Good question. The thing is, I didn't have a clue that this scene existed in my own back yard until I was treated to my first show (more on that in just a minute).

All you have to do is fire up your computer and do a little looking around. If you live near a major city, there is a good chance that you have a few of these bands in your neck of the woods. This is a lot like anything else regarding your conscious awareness. Once you put it on your radar, it will jump out at you. Suddenly, you have a list of a dozen bands to go see in places that you drove by every day and never gave a second thought.

While I can only speak from my personal experience, I have to believe that things are not going to be all that different in Portland, Maine than they are here in Portland, Oregon. And if you are a musician, maybe this will point you in a new and exciting direction.

As I share some of the moments and interviews I managed to collect during the creation of this book, I will also include some of the post-show reviews that I wrote up. I include these because I hope you will see something that inspires you to support these incredible entertainers. Yes, they are on stage. Yes, they are rock stars. But many of them are also insurance agents, construction workers, and dentists as well. They are not nearly as well paid as their namesakes and they rely on YOU to fill the house and join the party. And you already have something in common with them…you love the same music.

Now, on to the show…

***

Van Halen is one of those bands that arrived on the scene just as things were really starting to change in the world of music. They would incorrectly (in my opinion) be scooped up into a category known as the Hair Band.

With an over the top front man and a dynamic guitarist who would become a legend so much so that even his guitar would become an icon recognizable around the world, this band burned hot and blew up publically with MTV providing all the lurid details with both sides making inflammatory public claims as to where the blame should rest. They left behind a fan base that split just as strongly on a new incarnation.

Van Halen had a sound, and if you were fortunate to see them live in their glory days, you were treated to the equivalent of a musical circus with Diamond Dave as the boisterous ring master. However, what you also saw on many occasions was a front man who was sometimes too intoxicated (whether on fame or any number of rumored substances) to remember the words to those songs you came to hear.

Certainly nobody is perfect, and even the best can make a mistake, but this forgetfulness actually became part of the shtick. Mistakes are part of a live performance. Ask any performer about their most recent show and they will be able to tell you about every single error they committed—most going unnoticed by the audience, by the way. But with Van Halen, it was easy to spot those gaffs when words would be slurred, stumbled over, or just plain flubbed.

With fame, there is often a sense of complacency that can settle in and root itself deeply in those who have achieved a level of superstardom. I recall a certain bit of the Van Halen show that might have originated in some spontaneous moment, but eventually became part of every performance. The band would be cruising along and suddenly Dave would stop them. He would go on some rant about something being thrown up onto the stage and hitting him or one of the other members. He would get the crowd in a bit of a frenzy as he dressed down this mysterious offender, and then finish it up with the statement directed at this person (or one to the basic effect) of how "tonight, I'm gonna fuck your girlfriend!"

Believe it or not, the crowd usually cheered this with wild abandon. Yes, Dave would teach that jerk a lesson. By the fourth time in as many shows where I heard this spiel, I figured it out for what it was: part of the show.

So, what does any of that have to do with Tribute Bands? I guess it depends on what you want from live music. Personally, I come to see songs that I love being performed. It is hypnotic in a way to watch fingers fly over frets boards, drumsticks blurring and spinning. Live music kicks ass. I guess that is really the point that I am trying to make.

If I want to see and/or hear somebody botch up the songs I love from a par-ticular artist, I can just set up my camera to shoot video of myself. Why pay to watch others do it, right?

Tribute Bands try very hard to give the audience the best experience possi-ble. They strive to nail every note. Sure, anybody who has performed live will tell you that they never have a perfect performance, but you do see a level of quality with Tribute Bands that can often be missing in the real deal. For one, it is rare that you will find the members of a Tribute Band hitting the stage in a drunken stupor. Audiences would never stand for it and they would be off the circuit in a hurry. Clubs and other venues that put on these shows want to see high caliber entertainment that make people want to spend money...not walk out the door in disgust.

If you find some of your local acts in the Tribute scene, I would make the suggestion that you seek out their social media pages. Often, they will have in-formation on not only upcoming shows, but also how you can get tickets on the cheap. Many of Portland's bands get a fistful of service charge-free tickets that they are looking to sell.

Recently, my wife and I wanted to take my daughter to see Motorbreath, a Metallica Tribute Band. It is no secret that my wife thinks the world of the drummer, Joe Spencer. Yes, she loves the band. She thinks all of the guys are simply amazing; but the first time she saw Joe destroy a six-pack of sticks in one song, she had a crush. When she contacted the singer and guitarist, Kevin Staley, he told her she had to "get her tickets from her boyfriend."

As I said earlier, many of these bands go to the trouble of getting out there and meeting their fans. They let the audience know that they matter. During my interview session with the Motorbreath quartet, I let slip my wife's initial "OMG" reaction to watching the drummer during their opening number. Months later and numerous interactions in person and via social media later, the singer made my wife smile with his comment.

Being accessible to their audience is still not a good enough reason to see a Tribute Band. You need to be swept up in the sound. It needs to have that fa-miliar ring that seeps into the crevices of your memory and hooks you.

The following is the actual text of the review that I wrote after my first ex-perience seeing Unchained:

"I am a known KISS fan, but if I had to pick my top five bands of all time (excluding Stevie Ray Vaughn—he is his own category...GENIUS!), it would be:

1. *KISS*
2. *Van Halen (the DLR years...I was VERY unhappy when Sammy joined)*
3. *Aerosmith*

4. *Queensryche*
5. *Mötley Crüe*

So, seeing Unchained was a treat. These guys go the extra mile to pull off the tribute. "Eddie" keeps that ever-present smile, "Diamond Dave" is all swagger and innuendo, "Michael Anthony" carries killer harmony vocals and has a gruff sort of swagger, and "Alex" beats his drum kit with abandon.

Even better was how they pulled off the sound. Looks only get you so far, but Unchained leaves little doubt that you just re-lived the Van Halen experience. These guys are a blast...we were VERY close to the action. Which was almost like re-living my old days as a concert rat back in the 80's, minus having to sleep in the parking lot of the Portland Memorial Coliseum (which is what you had to do if you wanted to be up close on the floor back in the days of General Admission).

After the show, the band was even nice enough to pose for a few pics, and even brought along their Unchained Girls. Talk about making a guy feel special for his birthday. Diamond Dave even took home a copy of DEAD: The Ugly Beginning *and we talked briefly about the "good old days" of Romero's original* Dawn of the Dead. *Does a band get much cooler? Probably not."*

(I know that much of this seems familiar to what you just read in the first chapter. It is funny, but that is just the degree of effect the scene had on me. It drove something into my head. As I share it with you, I hope that you will feel some of the magic. Also, I am hoping that perhaps an aspiring Tribute Band artist might pick this up and glean something helpful.)

From that day forward, I would start seeking out these acts and becoming better acquainted with them and the scene they are a part of. Somehow, I continue to be surprised when I meet others who are not aware of this phenomenon. How soon I have forgotten about my own ignorance.

I realize that some will think that this book is becoming a very long stalker-boy love letter to the guys of Unchained. Maybe. But this is the band that took me by storm and made me want to find the other bands. So, in a way, they are like that first kiss.

It was almost six months and perhaps a half a dozen shows later when I committed to the idea I was entertaining in regards to wanting to write about these bands. And the final bell tolled at (wait for it...) an Unchained show. The band was going to perform the entire first Van Halen album in song order and its glorious entirety for the first half of the show.

It is always good to hear those favorite hits, but when the 80's metal scene was in its peak, you grabbed the album or cassette and listened to the entire thing. Yes, you usually liked the songs that made it to radio, but there was always that one track that you loved that you could not believe did not make it to the Top 40 playlist. On the first Van Halen album, that track was *Little Dreamer*.

So, here were my impressions of that show:

"It was like stepping into Mr. Peabody's Way Back Machine. The club was small and the crowd was anxious. Unlike my very first time seeing Van Halen live, I went into this show WITH expectations. After the opening act exited, I stood at the lip of the stage and waited for that sound...the blaring of car horns that signaled the start of the first Van Halen album as well as the start of this show.

The beauty of a live show is in its imperfection, and the night started with a test of Unchained and their ability to overcome as they blew the power twice in the first three numbers. True to form "Diamond Dave" simply used the glitch to play with the crowd.

The strains of RUNNIN' WITH THE DEVIL fade when it was time for "Shreddy Van Halleck" to fly into ERUPTION. That is a piece that will make or break a Van Halen tribute band. What makes Unchained special is how each member has worked to really personify the roles of the people they portray. Down to that trademark smile, Unchained's Eddie is something special to behold.

As Unchained shook off the early power issues, the band put on a show that could have stood by itself with JUST the set consisting of that first album being played from start to finish. Without a doubt, this band rates as one of (if not outright) my favorites in the "Tribute Band" scene.

Having caught my share, I can say that it takes more than just a wig and some Spandex. People seeing these bands are usually big fans of the original group. The tribute band can't get away with being so wasted that the music suffers...they have to nail the sound and feel of the band they portray if they want to win over the audience. By the time they played ON FIRE, they owned the crowd.

After a brief break, they returned in new costumes that gave that 80's vibe and launched into a set from the remaining Roth-led collection of VH. What makes Unchained so special is that they give all the bluster and bombast of the band they assume the identity of while making each member of the audience feel as if they are being performed for individually. "Alex" holds the band in time with his tight rhythm. "Eddie" smiles and makes eye contact with fans who are watching in rapt amazement as one of their guitar gods comes to life before their eyes. "Michael Anthony" stalks the stage with his bass and belts out the backing vocals like his real life counterpart. And you are so close that you can touch them. But don't worry, "Diamond Dave" will flirt, touch, tickle and cavort with anybody he can reach. At one point, he actually came out because, as he told the rabid audience, he wanted "to see what it looks like from out there with all you crazy people!"

By the end of the show, the audience was hot, sweaty, and happy. Unchained delivered the goods with interest. What makes them stand out is their dedication to putting on a great show and making the audience feel like it matters.

Having seen Unchained before, I wanted to add a few observations. It is obvious that the band has been focusing their energy on being better with each show. The backing vocals were polished and it is apparent that they have been either in vocal training or simply practicing very hard. "Michael Anthony" had a few moments where he was able to truly shine as he carried a solo line or two of the chorus on some of the songs.

If you are in the Portland area, I highly suggest that you catch these guys at any of their future shows. If you were/are a fan of the DLR era, these guys will give you more than your money's worth. If you search just a little, you might very well find your favorite band being given the Tribute treatment. Get out there and show some love.

3

Jason has a Formula

Back in the 80s, the Portland concert scene was largely "brought to you by the John Bauer Concert Promotions." When you heard that in an advertisement, it meant the Memorial Coliseum was gonna be rockin' hard.

These days, the music scene seems to be a fractured mess. The Tribute Band scene is lucky to have a promoter that knows what it takes to not only put a band in front of an audience, but (and this is perhaps more important) put an audience in front of a band.

Jason Fellman is the man behind J-Fell Presents and undoubtedly the most active person in the business and behind some of the best shows in the area. You may think that a promoter is not an exciting or interesting aspect of the music biz, much less an integral part of making it grow. Then you have obviously never met Jason Fellman.

If it helps any, he is also the drummer for Stone in Love, a Journey Tribute Band, and hands down the area's most successful as well as sought after band in the Tribute scene. Jason is also the mastermind behind what has become the J-Fell concert crown jewel, Harefest—a two-day outdoor music festival extravaganza featuring as many as sixteen bands that come on and off the stage with precision and flawless transition.

This event has become so big that it needed a change in venue to allow more attendees. The 2015 show which featured such acts as Motorbreath (Metallica), Shoot to Thrill (AC/DC), Petty Fever (Tom Petty), and of course Unchained (Van Halen) was able to accommodate 3000 people each day. It has allowances for on-site camping and a variety of food, beverage, and merchandise vendors who all looked to be doing a brisk business.

There are major recording artists that would love to play in front of a crowd that size, and Jason Fellman has made it almost a dream-come-true event for the acts that are fortunate enough to be booked for this epic show. On that day, these bands see a throng of fans that go so beyond what you might find in a small club or bar. It is a day that they truly get to live a performer's dream.

Jason Fellman is "the Ambassador of Good Times" for fans of live rock-and-roll. It is not a title that comes without a lot of hard work behind the scenes. He might be the head of J-Fell Presents, but he does not really consider himself a promoter in the usual sense. His rise to what must arguably be considered the area's best promoter of Tribute Bands (my label, not his) came from his desire to perform.

When I asked him about his role as promoter, he said, "I'm not really a booking agency or a talent agency, it's like more of an undefined entity that does booking and promotions…everything I do is driven by "where do I want to be as a musician." The genesis of doing Tribute Bands in the first place was that I felt like if I wanted to get the type of show and those types of opportunities [that] I wanted, I was going to have to create an environment in which to do that…that's the definition of marketing…creating an environment in which to sell. When I entered the market with our own product, it wasn't there…yet."

From those beginnings, Fellman put Stone in Love, his Journey Tribute Band, into action. His lineup is polished and has performed not only in clubs and some upscale venues, but also at corporate outings and many other events that allowed him to see that there was a demand for something familiar in the live music scene. People wanted to see a band take the catalog from one artist and put on a show consisting of the songs they knew and loved from their younger years.

He already had success with his 80's cover band, Radical Revolution, which plays a collection of pop hits from a variety of artists from that era. Stone in Love would be his launch into something very similar, but still remarkably different. The only thing now was to find some other people who were doing the Tribute Band show and doing it well. He would need to start seeking out other bands in order to create a roster of talent that bring in not just a handful of people interested in seeing a show, but actual crowds that would make bigger and better venues sit up, take notice, and then call on J-Fell to line up the talent.

The bands he brings in are varied. He sees himself as more of a coach for these acts than he does a promoter in the traditional sense.

Fellman: "A typical promoter will just fill in dates. 'I got five dates, I need five shows. I got a venue that's empty, I gotta put in shows.' I'm looking at things where I have 'X' number of bands and each band needs to have a promoted show 'X' number of times a year. So, I almost look at it like a planning matrix."

All the bands under the J-Fell banner receive their shows in quality locations. After that, if they play in other locations on their own—that is up to the artists—but once he has them, they know they will see bookings in quality locations.

Let's face it, we have all been to places that we'd just as soon never visit again. I have gone to a few locales to see some of my favorites and felt like I needed two showers afterwards. There are some houses that really have no business putting on a concert-style show. From soundboard operators who haven't a clue, to crowds that are more interested in their own conversations than in listening to the music, club bands have some rough gigs. J-Fell knows those places and will not book there.

For Fellman, it is a process to seek out the acts that make up his roster. He doesn't just look for any Tribute Band; he has a method to his madness. What follows is his check-off list. These items are in no particular order, but they make up the Fellman Formula. So, if you are a Tribute Band looking to find a slot on the J-Fell roster, consider this your own cheat sheet.

Jason Fellman (J-Fell Presents): "First, it is the quality of the band, the actual product...the total product quality. I don't separate...they are either compelling to go see, or they're not. [And] it's really obvious. People go see them, and react. The chances are, if there is a Tribute Band, and they are not getting traction, it's not a marketing or promotional problem...some Tribute Bands trade more on energy, some on authenticity.

"The second thing is whether the band actually promotes and has a good stream of energy flowing from the band. I'm not looking to be a surrogate promoter for a band. You're talking about a $15 ticket. Nobody is going to make a lot of money on that...not me, and not the band. Part of the reason that I use the analogy of [being a] coach is that most local bands generally have the natural resources they need to draw...bands can develop *social capital*. If they know two fans in the audience who don't know each other and then introduce them to each other you have created social capital in the form of goodwill around your band. Those two people meet each other and form a relationship, the context of that relationship is the band...I have ZERO interest in working with bands who are not excited about this, if I am more excited about the band than they are, then there is really no reason to talk about it anymore. That said, some bands can get away with not being super-aggressive promoters if they are passionate about their product."

Item three in this list is perhaps one of the biggest parts when you consider the ingredients to this rock and roll promoter's recipe. After all, a Tribute Band can be stacked with amazing musicians and have all the talent and presence in the world, but if they are paying tribute to perhaps a one-hit-wonder like say Aldo Nova, Faster Pussycat, Autograph, or Giant, you are simply not going to pack the house.

Fellman: "The third thing I am looking at is the viability of the source material. In general, I take ten percent of where the actual band plays or would play if they were to tour today. So, for example…Journey plays at the Rose Garden [Moda Center]. What's it seat, around 20,000? Stone in Love would likely cap out *selling* 2,000 tickets. This has nothing to do with how good the Tribute Band is…'niche' bands don't get it, why I don't want to work with them…there is nothing I can do with them. I could put you on a bill, but you would *always* be the opening band. It's unfortunate, but if your goal is to play for large audiences, don't pick an obscure band to cover."

Since that initial interview, Fellman has had to adjust a few things in his role as promoter. In a follow-up session, he shared how much things have changed in just the one year since our first sit-down interview.

Fellman: "I've changed my model a little bit. In past years when my roster was a little bit smaller and the Tribute scene was on the way up, if you were on my roster, then that meant I was going to promote all your local shows…you're gonna have 'X' number of shows per year in quality venues. That has become unsustainable for several reasons. One, that supply/demand curve that we talked about getting out of whack (a year ago) when we did this interview…it's now completely out of whack. It's really difficult for bands to go and play at larger venues…there are only so many combinations of Van Halen, Scorpions, The Cult and so on that I can put forth to the public. Demand is still growing, but at a slower rate than the supply. Meanwhile, the number of Tribute Bands has just gone through the roof. And now the 90's bands are coming online. The new model is centered around using this draw to negotiate more favorable deals in the best clubs. There are some criteria that must be met in these places: a good PA, good lights, and they staff a sound person (which is important). Being on my roster no longer means you're going to have 'X' number of shows. What it really means is that, I am out there looking out for your best interests and opportunities. Whether it is booking you at these special events or pitching the bands for corporate gigs…the coaching component is still the heart of it."

We discussed a number of corporate venues that are now seeking these bands for various functions. Places like Nike are asking for bands like Appetite for Deception and Unchained.

Love it or hate it, you can't deny his logic. After all, despite the goodwill that often exists in this area when it comes to the Tribute Band scene, it is still a business in many ways. If you want to fly under the banner of one of the best, you have to be ready to play by the J-Fell game plan. That brings us to his fourth ingredient: the somewhat ambiguous concept known as *social capital*.

"For starters, I have to be able to get along with the band. You know…honesty, communication."

Simple when you look at it. And Jason is not shy about pointing out that steady work (aka money) has an uncanny way of making "band problems" magically disappear. If everybody is making their fair share, it goes a long way to keeping everybody happy from the top to the bottom. He pointed out that it is important to clarify that money in and of itself does not solve everything, but that bands tend to focus on their problems when they are not working. When a band is active and busy…there is forward momentum and people are focusing on the right things.

He is very involved in seeing the Tribute Band scene grow. Stagnation does not help anybody, and Jason is always looking for something new to add to his roster that will spur growth. After all, he has his own band in this scene. If people start seeing quality Tribute Bands around town, then the hope is that they will become regulars to the scene and seek out others.

When I first sat down with him, he was very excited about a new act that he found. The group is called Grand Royale, and they are a Beastie Boys Tribute Band. Many of the acts currently playing had members that often belonged to more than one group. Grand Royale was entirely made up of new faces that had no ties to him or anybody that he knew. This would be a totally new batch of seven guys coming into the scene. Also, they were expanding the sound palate.

The majority of the acts in the Portland scene were hard rock, hair metal, and that sort. To bring in a Beastie Boys Tribute Band would add an entirely new layer to the bean dip. This would also mean seven guys with their own new relationships and networks entering the scene. This would be the growth that Fellman was looking for. To welcome these guys to the roster, J-Fell booked a show sandwiching Grand Royale between Unchained as the opener and Shoot to Thrill as the closer. Fast forward just a few months and Grand Royale was taking the stage at Harefest 5.

That brings me to what must be considered the crown jewel of the J-Fell calendar. Harefest is an outdoor music festival. It takes place in Canby, Oregon. For two days and nights, the stage belongs to some of the best Tribute Bands around. In 2016, Harefest 6 consists of the following bands:

1. Stone in Love – Journey
2. Aerosmith rocks – Aerosmith
3. Steelhorse – Bon Jovi
4. Grand Royale – Beastie Boys
5. Lovedrive – Scorpions
6. Same Ol' Situation – Mötley Crüe
7. Sonic Temple – The Cult
8. Appetite for Deception – Guns-n-Roses
9. Barracuda – Heart
10. Shoot to Thrill – AC/DC

11. Ramble On – Led Zeppelin
12. Motorbreath – Metallica
13. All Fired Up – Pat Benatar
14. Plush – Stone Temple Pilots
15. Unchained – Van Halen
16. Jukebox Heroes – Foreigner

Seriously, how could anybody who loves live music and good old rock-and-roll pass up seeing a show with a lineup like that? Harefest harkens back to the days of old in the concert world. Shows like Oregon Jam, Day on the Green, and the US Festival. Are there still big music festivals? Sure. But besides costing an arm and a leg, they usually consist of a lot of acts you have never heard of.

Granted, these are Tribute Bands, but in many cases, you will be hard pressed to tell the difference. I highly suggest that you cruise over to J-Fell.com and surf around. Sign on to the mailing list and see for yourself. Check out a few shows.

When you do, this chapter about the man that is making a big difference in the Tribute scene will resonate perhaps just a bit stronger.

4

Stone in Love: Blueprint for Success

There are a lot of groups representing a wide variety of music styles. The most successful act in the Portland area when it comes to sheer numbers of attendees and the venues they fill has to be the Journey Tribute Band, Stone in Love.

Journey is one of those bands that crosses over to cover a wide variety of music tastes. Those who remember Journey at the apex of its Steve Perry era know what I mean. There is a lot to their music, and it is the subtleties that made that band so great. To take on such a diverse act that sported one of the most iconic voices in pop rock of the 80's is a challenge all by itself. Add the complexity of Neal Schon's guitar work and the task is daunting indeed.

The members of Stone in Love take what they do very seriously, and have to be seen as a blueprint for success in the Tribute Band scene. Sitting down with the band, you quickly pick up on a very diverse set of personalities. What could be a recipe for disaster is actually the reason that this band continues to excel and has kept the same lineup since inception.

One of the first decisions that group needs to make is what group they are going to have as their focus. Refer back to Jason Fellman's points about how it is best to choose a band that has wide appeal. That seemed like the best place to start when I sat down with the members of Stone in Love. The question: Why Tribute Bands in the first place, and why Journey?

Kevin Hahn (vocals): "I think we loved the music first. Personally for me, it's like my first love…first concert, first band I could really remember being into, first record I could really remember being into and it just really made a great impression on me. For me, as a singer, I can really identify, and the music really resonates. For me, when I'm on stage singing, it's just natural, organic…ya know? The money is not the thing…it's nice, but this won't work if we didn't enjoy it."

Davin (lead guitar): "I mostly just lucked into it because of a drunken conversation with these two {motions in the direction of Hahn and Mike Johnson}. Kevin would sing karaoke, and he would always get requests to do Journey. So he and Mike (keyboards) would always joke about doing that. We all met because Jason (drummer) had done an album with Kevin. Kevin would come up and sing in our 80's cover band {Radical Revolution}. He would do the Journey songs. I just happened to be in the middle of that circle. Right place...right time for me."

Dain Ryan (bass): "I got a text message from Mike at about two in the morning telling me about this guy (Hahn). The next night, I get a call and Mike says, "Journey Tribute Band." Working with these guys, we were all (already) so close. It's really cool to work with your buddies."

Mike Johnson (keyboards): "Yeah, it started with the karaoke and this joke about when we were going to start our Journey Tribute Band. Then it turned into this funny conversation that went on for over a year. We literally went to Journey one time in the Gorge. We were doing the 80's cover band already with Jason and we had this circle of guys between what we all played that fit the part. I'm not a keyboard player by nature, I play bass most of the time, but the thought was that 'Wow, we could really make this work.' We joke about how this could have been two gigs (at Dante's) and then been over...but here we are, five years later...tax debt. {Group laughter}"

Jason Fellman (drummer): "For me ultimately it was just a manifestation of my desire to play drums (in this case), play music I like with people I like for as big of an audience as possible of people who will enjoy it. Ultimately, for me personally, it's just one of those bands that meets all my musical goals...people know the music and it's cool."

I managed to see Stone in Love at a groovy little place in Portland called Doug Fir Lounge. You go downstairs into this well-insulated room where the sound is surprisingly good. The music really is showcased here, and I highly suggest catching a show at this venue if you are able. Here is what I had to say about that night:

"Yep, it was another one of those weekends where, unless you were with me, you missed out on something amazing. Like my favorite ghoul, Ava Birch, I have a love for all things 80s. And while I was more often found at the Judas Priest and Van Halen Concerts, I also had/have a love for groups like Journey, Styx, and Foreigner. Journey was "kissin' music". Seriously, if you went to high school in the early 80s, then you know exactly what I am saying.

"I saw these guys at Harefest this summer, but to be able to experience them up close in a more intimate venue (GREAT JOB to the folks at The Doug Fir Lounge) was a treat. Stone in Love is not only spot on in the sound of their talented musicians, but in the most important and difficult place...VOCALS. I

defy most men to try and nail the sound if Steve Perry. My voice cracks just thinking about it. But once you hear Kevin, you will be transported to those glory days of the power ballad. And, fellas, it is normal to be jealous. Seriously, I was surrounded by a throng of women (from 21 to 61) who wanted to take him home and have their way. Simply put, his voice is butter. He had them eating out of his hand from the moment he took the stage with all that energy and started in on Separate Ways (Worlds Apart).

"And all of that is fine, but it means nothing if the band does not pull their weight. Trust me...they do. The guitar work was stellar and the timing being kept by bass and drums were stellar. I was also impressed with the backing vocals. A lot of times, that gets dialed down to almost inaudible, but the band really holds their own. That is most apparent with the song "Anytime." And as a side note, the drummer is a blast to watch. It is obvious that he loves what he is doing. I am reminded of John Mayer. If you have ever seen Mayer perform, you know he is into it by watching his face...same goes with Jason Fellman, drummer for Stone in Love.

"The band nails every aspect of the Journey sound. So, if you are a fan, I suggest checking out their website, Facebook page, or the J-Fell Presents page for the next show date info. Besides Stone in Love, you will find a number of other amazing acts to catch and the venues where you will find them."

It was easy to see why this band is in such high demand when it comes to quality Tribute Bands in the area; they specialize in festivals and corporate gigs and have actually managed to outgrow the bar and club scene. Yes, they can rock, but it is not the ear-piercing, heavily distorted sound that you find with the harder groups that play.

As I watched and observed the crowd, you would be hard pressed to convince yourself that the actual band (from the 80's) was not up on the stage. Not only was the sound tight, but the women up front did everything in their power to try and reach out and simply touch singer Kevin Hahn. He never missed a beat, even when very politely peeling his hand from the grasp of an eager female fan.

I had the chance to ask him about that and he said, "You know, overall, I'm just appreciative of people's energy. But you do have to retain your concentration. That's that whole thing of not getting swept up. Like, you have to hold your ground because it's just pretty crazy energy-wise you know with the whole everybody wanting to get your attention in that way. Like "Sing to me!" and I think that goes to I appreciate [how] everyone has their own musical experience. For us, we're just in a lucky position to be able to do that and give that to the audience...every show is kinda crazy and you almost get used to it now. I just try to do what we do, focus, and do what we're supposed to do. The craziness is just like a normal thing."

Being able to talk with this band was revealing, and there is a lot to be shared not only for fans of this group, but any person looking to start up a Tribute Band. They know how to capture an audience and then enthrall them as much as the band to which they pay tribute.

That single question and response set of a conversation between the band members about staying focused and how, while mistakes happen with live performances since nobody is perfect, they have yet to experience anything that could be considered a "train wreck" while performing. Again, that speaks to the levels of professionalism that each member of this band holds himself to as a performer and musician.

Despite their talent, the reality is that they are playing in venues that put the audience much closer than you might find at a stadium gig. The security is simply not in place to keep the people at a distance. This allows for things that include fans insisting that they be allowed up to sing with the band—something you can likely not even imagine happening at an actual Journey concert.

As Hahn put it at one point during that discussion, "You have to remember up there that this is *your* (meaning his and the band's) show. You have a responsibility to the show."

This is the beauty of the Tribute Band scene, but it can also be a curse. Not every band out there has the ethic and professionalism that you find with the members of Stone in Love. The music scene is really like any other job in that way. There are those who want to simply show up and collect a check, and then there are those who take pride in what they do. If a band is making it look easy, chances are, they are one of the former versus the latter, and the five members of Stone in Love make it look like a breeze. Considering that many of them are playing instruments that are their "second" choice or in a style they were not entirely used to, that says something about the talent that takes the stage anytime Stone in Love takes the stage.

Unlike many of the Tribute Bands that strive to capture the visual look of their namesake, Stone in Love simply allows their music to do all the talking. They admittedly do play it a bit faster than Journey's studio tempo, but the sound does not suffer, and it might even allow them to fit in that one extra hit to make the audience that much happier.

When asked about their secret to success, Fellman replied, "We have a really solid product coupled with the right time."

Johnson added, "I think the biggest is you have to somehow make it your own. What I mean by that is that what's going on onstage has to be real. You have to truly enjoy what's going on. For me it's like it would all be worthless if I wasn't believable or if the band wasn't believable, especially like the vocal thing. That's a huge thing."

Fellman went on to say, "Energy, enthusiasm, and a connection with the music will carry the day every time."

With a band this popular in the scene, it seemed only right to ask them what advice they had for other bands working their way up the ladder and seeking the level of booking success that they have achieved.

Fellman: "The first thing you have to look at is the source material. There are certain bands where you just have to align your expectations to it. If you are doing a tribute to a band that only has two or three hits or maybe even only five [hits], it's just never gonna headline anything bigger than maybe a three hundred-person venue, if that. The number one factor is the source material. It's easy to hit a home run when you're starting on third base. And you have to get over yourself. It's such a big deal, getting wrapped up on what the poster is going to look like, what is the band order gonna be, and what's the percentage breakdown on the tickets. It's amazing how much…you know…making things difficult for the promoter. If they [I] have to spend a bunch of time re-communicating things, chasing down photos, checking calendars, that is time not spent promoting. So another one is to just have your act together. We did not create the template of what a professional band looks like, we just followed it. Most bands succeed or fail in spite of themselves. In this market (I hate to say it). Ninety percent of the songs in a Tribute Band set list should be the biggest hits the band had [has]."

Davin: "You have to have a good singer to front the band. All the business aside, it's not gonna matter if you don't have a good singer…and a band that can actually draw. Then you get the players. In this town, at this point, you can get players."

This might all seem like basic common sense, yet bands come and go every single day. Lineups change and groups continuously struggle to find that one magic piece of the puzzle to take them to the next level. Just like that set of keys you put on the table and then passed over ten times as you searched frantically for them later, the answer can often be right in front of your face; but do you have the vision to see it?

We wrapped up with just a brief conversation about where these men felt the future of the Tribute Band scene might be headed.

Davin: "It is completely up to the bands at this point. It is a trend that you would think should have run its course, but since the bands are actually starting to get better, I don't know. Is it getting too popular…it feels like a stock market run at this point where everybody is making a Tribute Band which does diminish…it meant something when there was only four of them and you could name who the four were. Now there [are] six million people introduced to the market. Whether they get a good experience the first time out, who knows. If they see a really good one like Appetite [for Deception—Guns-n-Roses Tribute Band] and are like "Wow! This is amazing; I want to see more of it." Or have we come to the place where we've actually hit…we've gotten the radio involved so we may be tapping out the pyramid. There may not be much more base to find, in which case it's a matter of can the bands keep producing more interesting and accurate portrayals."

Fellman: The supply is definitely increasing at a faster rate than the demand.

Ryan: "Nothing lasts forever."

Davin: "That being said, it could fan out two ways. It doesn't mean the end of Tributes, it just means it will weed out all the weak ones…it will reset the market for a while."

Johnson: "I can honestly see us doing this ten years from now. I think one of the biggest things is the demographics; our listeners are like thirty, forty, fifty. After a certain while, people are going to stop going out."

Fellman: "There are also two different markets. So you have to look at it two different ways. To what end are people going to stop going out to shows each weekend. The other is the market for what we do [three shows a year] that you can buy tickets to basically. The other shows we do are things like Summer Concert series or fairs and festivals…corporate events and stuff like that. That part of the market will sustain itself for a lot longer. The thing about Journey is that it is appealing to the sweet spot of about 35-55, so we've probably got about another ten years or so where it's going to be appealing to a corporate decision maker. We will probably get tired of doing it before the band fades [or one of us, it's just inevitable…my hands could go]."

One other factor is that magical dividing line between the 80's and the 90's. There can be no denying that the live music scene and music as a whole really changed during that time. Concerts were more of an event back then versus the commercialized business that they have become. The availability of being able to see your band on YouTube or some social media platform was not part of the 80's reality. That added to the excitement and the mystique which has been stripped away.

Just a note when it comes to social media and YouTube in particular when it comes to Stone in Love. This band has reached such a prestigious status when it comes to nailing the Journey sound (coupled with the new singer for the current Journey lineup featuring a talented singer of Asian heritage much like Hahn of Stone in Love) the band Journey has demanded that Stone in Love videos be removed from sites like YouTube.

5

Motorbreath Rises

I was at the Hawthorne Theater for a show one night. Honestly, I can't recall who all was on that bill as I sit down to begin this chapter, perhaps the script from my review later will be helpful in that regard. What is important is the impression I received that evening.

Much like a first kiss, you don't get a second chance to make a first impression. Seeing Motorbreath for the first time is still seared into my mind. There was a fury and a presence that caught me completely off guard.

The band took the stage and wasted no time getting hard and heavy. Yet, I missed a good part of the first number. Why? Because my wife elbowed me in the ribs and pointed to the drummer. I will get back to that in just a moment. As for the show as a whole, it was amazing.

That night, they pulled members of the audience up on stage to "give them a hand" with their closing number, *Seek and Destroy*. After pulling about a dozen eager fans up, the band tore into that final song and Staley shared the mic with a mixture ranging from the shy and timid, to the visibly intoxicated, to the amazed fan who could not believe that they were being allowed to share in living a dream-come-true for that single moment in time. When it was over, I felt I had a basic grasp on the four very different and unique members.

Drummers are much like bass players in most bands. They are the engine that drives the machine; but they can often go unnoticed. By the end of the first song, Motorbreath drummer, Joe Spencer, had destroyed perhaps a half a dozen drum sticks. Yet, through it all, he never missed a beat. It was like seeing a human incarnation of the Muppet drummer Animal. Teamed with bass player Mark Trees, the engine that would keep the time and maintain the frenetic pace of such stalwart Metallica musts as *Master of Puppets*, *For Whom the Bell Tolls*, and mainstream hit *Enter Sandman* worked like a very well-oiled machine.

Pulling off the two guitar attack that the band is known for is a feat unto itself and guitarists Kevin Staley and Bob Capka proved up to the task. To shred with such amazing timing is yet another skill that many bands fall short in pulling off with such mastery.

The Hetfield vocals performed by Staley were infused with just enough growl and attitude. Here is an excerpt from the review I wrote in regards to that triple bill I caught featuring the fearsome foursome that make up Motorbreath:

"Saturday I went to see a concert featuring the tribute bands Lovedrive, Unchained, and Motorbreath. It was a time travel experience as I was transported to metal's glory days. If I closed my eyes, you could not convince me I was not hearing the Scorpions, Van Halen, and Metallica...The last band to hit the stage was Motorbreath. That put the audience into a moshing frenzy. And this is not a band that just plays the radio friendly hits of the group's more popular hits with the average Joe. Nope...they want to shred your ears with the songs that TRUE Metallica fans love (Denise and I still had ringing in our ears late Sunday night). And the amount of energy and fury that you will witness just can't be put into words. If you just spend the night watching the drummer (like Denise...she has a husband-approved fangirl crush on Motorbreath's drummer), you will witness a passion that the actual Metallica band has lost long ago...The Motorbreath set was an in-your-face onslaught of Metallica that should come with a warning label stating that if you are not ready to rock, perhaps you should go home and listen to your Barry Manilow records...This was an amazing show from start to finish. So, once again, I have to tell you, search around your local music scene. In Portland, you don't have to look far for an experience that you will never forget. And when was the last time you saw Scorpions, Van Halen, or Metallica and then the band came out into the crowd after the show and said hi? That is just one more element that makes this experience so unique. The band actually cares if you had a good time."

I would see them several more times. Each time out, I could see this band becoming more cohesive. This was one of those bands that went through a few lineups to get the perfect mix. It would now seem that they have found it. They have developed onstage personalities that, while paying tribute to metal masters Metallica, are unique and distinct. Their becoming headliners in the Tribute Band scene is a testament to not only the talent each possess, but also an undeniable onstage chemistry. My last impression of them before the 2016 Harefest show would be from a performance at the Doug Fir Lounge that took place almost a year after my first experience seeing these guys.

"This past Saturday, another great combo was unleashed on the public. Jason Fellman of J-Fell Presents brought together a musical taste sensation that left all those in attendance hungry for more. This was my first time seeing Plush

(a Stone Temple Pilots Tribute Band). Now, I can't claim to be a huge STP guy, but I know the hits, and they played them with enough flash to impress. I will look forward to seeing these guys again. How can I not love a band where the drummer is wearing a classic "KISS Originals" tee shirt? The set was solid from top to bottom and featured a guest appearance by Motorbreath's own incarnation of Muppet Animal, Joe Spencer doing some backing vocals! That is one of the beautiful things about this scene. Many of these guys know each other, support each other at each other's venues, and are not hung up on themselves to the point of feeling like they can't bring a fellow performer up to whip the crowd into a fervor.

"Still, I can't lie and deny that the reason I ventured out on a cold, rainy Saturday was to see Motorbreath. Fronted by Kevin Staley, this group brings you Metallica in its raw glory. If you were at the Doug Fir this past Saturday, then you saw four men who exude a love for what they are doing. And if you hung out after, you may have even heard one member admit to being uncharacteristically nervous about playing such an amazing gig.

"Kevin Staley was at his gritty best on vocals. But beyond that talent, he fronts the band with a smile plastered on his face like he is living a waking dream. He hammers at his guitar and makes jokes with the crowd. He is not shy about getting close to the audience, and makes every attendee in the room feel like they are his personal guest. Whether you have seen them once or a dozen times, you get a new show with Kevin. He really shines on Master of Puppets *as he draws the crowd into the refrain again and again to the point you almost never want the song to end.*

"Mark Trees on bass looks like a bouncer who came up and snatched the guttural instrument away from whomever else might have dared to play it. He will cast a menacing scowl one moment, and then smile like he is everybody's best friend the next. He does a superb job as part of the rhythm engine that drives the band. Spend just one song following him around on stage with your eyes. He is all the expression you might expect from Gene Simmons in full makeup. You never doubt for a moment that he loves where he is at that moment.

"Bob Capka (I had the pleasure of working with his dad in the early 90's at a sports radio station) is the mystery man of the bunch. His guitar is superbly played through every single song, and he is amazing to watch, but he never seems to try and plant a flag in the spotlight to take you away from the show. It isn't like he hides, he just does not go overboard and upstage the band. His amazing guitar work is extremely impressive, but you actually find yourself looking for him at times. This might seem bad, or a slight, but it is exactly the opposite. A lot of guitarists with his talent might try to be constantly center stage, sucking in as much of the crowd's attention as possible, but Capka simp-

ly plays a damn good guitar and brings you along for the ride.

"I saved Joe "Animal" Spencer for last. Not because he is "just the drummer", but because he is absolutely amazing to watch. If you notice, I don't have a picture of him in action. That is because he is a blur of movement, and very hard to capture on film. Bring a camera capable of fast shutter speeds if you want to stop this man in time for a moment. It was his drumming that first caught not only my eye, but that of the missus. My wife thinks the world of Joe, not only as a drummer, but as a person. But back to his performance. Recently, I posted a video of this band playing For Whom the Bell Tolls. *Just watch it and tell me what comes to your mind. Much like Bothan spies in* Star Wars, *"many sticks and drum heads were lost to bring you this Motorbreath performance."*

This is one of those bands that has no need to try and look like their namesake. What matters most is the sound. Metallica fans are the sort that know every lilt and phrase to every lead and solo. This is a band that relies on the guitarist in a big way. That is not to say that the vocals are not an integral part, but if the guitars are botched, then there is going to be problems in building the fan base.

Also, the drumming is massive and fills a great deal of the sound. Lars Ulrich builds layers of complexity under the wall of guitars that scream, wail, and gallop along. Tackling an icon is no easy feat.

Metallica is a band that has a very distinct sound. Couple that with a fiercely loyal fan base and anybody who dares to tread down this path had best be dedicated to doing it right. Motorbreath appears to be very up for such a challenge.

The foursome that make up this band are from varying backgrounds that range from military ties to a union carpenter. As with other bands in the scene, they are not doing this with aspirations of massive wealth (although each agree it would not suck to be rich), they do this because they love to perform.

In addition to finding them on stage, it is very common to run into one, or even all of them in the audience of the shows being put on by other Tribute Bands. In that regard, they are as much fans of the scene as they are players in it.

I asked them about the prep they do on show day just out of curiosity since I have seen this band enough times to know that they leave it all up there and never give the audience a show that is half-assed.

Kevin Staley (guitars & vocals): "A lot of Echinacea and vitamin C…a lot of mental preparation just getting into the zone and being prepared. Making sure you got all your stuff…have a few brewskis and be really chill because it's a great group of guys that get along and everything just seems to be flawless every time we get together and do a show."

Bob Capka (guitars): "Hang out with my daughter since Dad's gonna be gone tonight…it's different and just depends on what I'm doing that day, but I don't really do much, I mean, to me…it's just another day and tonight's just another night that we get to rock."

Mark Trees (bass & backing vocals): "Sleep as late as possible, make sure I have a good breakfast."

Joe Spencer (drums): "I carb load, masturbate until air comes out, and stay hydrated as much as possible. And twenty minutes before…try to masturbate one more time and then stretch." (band laughter) and Staley adds, "He's not fucking joking either." (more laughter)

Now, I will take this moment to remind you that you are reading about rock stars. They may not be selling out 50,000 seat arenas and stadiums, but this is still the rock-and-roll culture. To that end, I never know what to expect when I sit down with these various bands. What I did find incredibly interesting was that I received a message from drummer Joe Spencer the following day after this interview saying that maybe some of his comments might have been seen by me as him being disrespectful. Nothing could be further from the truth. After all, I do think I have a decent sense of humor and am able to detect friendly jokes and general mischievousness. However, it struck me as just one more reason to further be impressed with Spencer and his depth of character. If a group of guys like this were to ever take itself too seriously (except for their devotion to the music) they would cease to be the entertaining showmen that I have come to admire and respect as performers.

[Author's note: I of course gave Spencer, as well as all of my interviewees, the chance to see this book prior to publication so that they could have anything stricken from the pages if they felt it might be misconstrued or cast them in a negative light. I am happy to include their unedited selves in these pages so that you might feel like you are getting to know these performers just a little bit better. Now, on with the show.]

To get a real feel for the Tribute Band mindset, I did ask this group of talented performers why they would want to do a Tribute Band instead of perhaps taking on the "original" scene such as it is.

Staley: "The reason I do this is because my dream of making it in the "big time" with my fucking original music is really over. It still happens on the side, but really, I have also come to the fact that I am forty-six years old, and you know what? I'm playing music to people who'll feed it right back to me with the shit we grew up on. That's why I'm doing it. And plus, we make a little scratch on the side and it's fun as fuck! Bottom Line."

Capka: "And we get to play Metallica songs all night."

Staley: "We get to play Metallica, dude." (chorus of laughter and agreement from the whole band)

Capka: "I tour all over the world with Vicious Rumors. I play guitar with

31

VR, a band that has been around for about thirty-five years (from the Bay area). We play all over, and I tell ya, man, these Motorbreath shows are just as much fun…they really are, because the crowd's super into it. If you like Metallica, you should enjoy the show."

Spencer: "I was in a symphonic metal band when I first moved here and it was designed after Metallica's *S & M*. Basically heavy metal with a symphony behind it. We had an opera singer and a violin player composing these classical pieces, and it was just amazing…when I was eleven years old and the *Black Album* came out, it changed my life. It became my actual passion for music and it led me in the direction of what I wanted to do. I always wanted to play music because of Metallica. So, meeting these guys and getting invited in to play in the Metallica Tribute is more than a dream come true for me. I can go out there and pretend to be my hero (Lars Ulrich) every night or as often as we can do it. [And] I've loved these songs my whole life and I've played 'em my whole life…fourteen years old playing *Damage Inc.* (that would be *Damage Incorporated* for all those non-Metallica types out there) and I just love this music. And to go out and do it…it's not for the accolades. I've been playing this in my basement my whole life so there is nothing changing in my mentality when I go on stage from when I was fourteen years old. It's just as cool as it can ever be."

It is just that sort of passion that is shared by each and every single member of this band that makes seeing a Motorbreath show seem perhaps even better than catching their namesakes where you might be so far away from the stage that you are watching it more on the Jumbo Tron (which is basically reducing the experience to a TV show) than anything else. Also, this group will wade out into the crowd after the show and pose for pictures, shake hands, and thank *you* for being there; something that I can almost promise with certainty you will not get from the actual Metallica.

6

Days of Yore

The lights go down and there is that moment where the audience waits for that first screaming guitar or crash of drums. Every generation feels that their music was the best and we all mourn as the artists that created the soundtracks of our lives either quit or break up like so many bad marriages. Then they return, unfortunately, if you want to see them on that first (or tenth) reunion/farewell tour, it means taking out a second mortgage to afford the tickets.

Growing up in the 70's and 80's, naturally I feel like I was witness to some of the most epic live performances of all time. That is not to say there are not some great performers today, but with technology being what it is, you often have no idea how much of a performance is being played live and how much is canned. Computers operate lighting systems with military precision as flames, lasers, and even holographic images add to the atmosphere.

Music has almost taken a backseat to the spectacle and overwhelming barrage of special effects. One of the things that I discovered during the many Tribute Band shows that I attended was an abundance of extremely talented musicians. The reliance was on their ability to bring the audience back to something special. Not that there are not amazing stage shows with lights and fog, but those are really second to the music.

If you attend a Tribute Band performance, you might not always get bands that "look" exactly like their namesakes. Yes, there are a few acts out there that strive to not only recreate the sound, but they also seek to nail down that certain exterior image. With a band like KISS, that can be a much easier feat. Attempting it with bands like Guns N' Roses or Bon Jovi might be a bigger challenge; however, much as in real life…looks only get a person so far.

When a group of musicians get together and make the decision to choose a single band and stride down the path of Tribute versus cover band, they are choosing what can actually be a much more dangerous road when it comes to being successful.

Speaking to many of the performers, there seemed to be a general consensus. A standard cover band can get away with sounding similar and is not expected to really nail down a particular artist. That does not apply to a Tribute Band. The audience is coming in with expectations. In many cases, they know every lilt and phrase of not just the lyrics, but the guitars and perhaps even the rhythm engine of bass and drums as well.

Stepping into somebody else's shoes and claiming to pay tribute to an act means that you need to have the studio sound and quality that is imprinted on the hearts and minds of the people in the audience. Choosing to simply improv a solo versus nailing the note-for-note transcription that the original artist laid down can leave an audience feeling jaded.

It is one thing to go see the Van Halens, Ozzys, and Journeys of the world and hear those performers beef up a lick or even tweak the tempo of a beloved song. They created that piece, therefore, they can do whatever they like and most often the audience will go wild.

The 80's saw the rise of MTV. That allowed many people to finally see various artists not only aping it up in outlandish videos. (Who can forget the often exotic locales that were the backdrop for many of the Duran Duran hits!) It also brought live performance to the small screen in a way that had not been seen since the days of *Don Kirshner's Rock Concert*. An entire generation of music lovers grew up watching their rock heroes perform.

I paid a whopping $9.50 to see Van Halen on their *Unchained* tour. It was general admission back then, which meant camping out in the parking lot of the Memorial Coliseum for a few days in order to get close to the action. Being in the first row was a badge of honor during that time. There were no corporations buying out the first three rows and doling out the tickets to people who likely could not name a single song by the performers that was not a Top Ten hit. Nope, the front rows were for the crazy, unwashed fans that endured pouring rain or blazing sun as they slept (or passed out) on the asphalt while waiting in line. And did your eyes pop out of your head just a bit when you saw that ticket price? These days, that doesn't cover the service fee for most venues.

This is another reason that the Tribute Band scene is vastly superior in many ways to seeing the actual artist. You can often catch a show for between ten and fifteen bucks (with the exception of an event like Harefest which I will discuss later). The performers understand the love that their audience has for a particular act and often shares that love. (No, not always, but more often than not it seems to be the case from what I gathered during my interviews.) They know they have to be true to the sound you remember from those albums, cassettes, and {gasp!} 8-tracks.

As I have said, when you catch a quality Tribute Band, it is almost like stepping into a time machine. When the band takes the stage and you are surrounded by a room full of people who are likeminded fans with at least one thing in common (the love of the music being played that night), it can be a magical experience. Suddenly, you are not watching a handful of local guys in wigs, Spandex, and makeup; instead, you are watching that band from your youth. You are hearing that ONE song that you used to crank up full blast when you pulled out of the high school parking lot.

You are singing along with all those people packed in around you who are immersed in their own memories. You are creating a new memory with a friend, or maybe you are introducing one of your offspring to the music that "brought mom and dad together." This is the Tribute scene at its finest.

While this book was written in the Portland, Oregon region, it is a simple matter of doing a local search for Tribute Bands in your own area. Find the ones that are playing the music that you enjoy and then just go out and see them. The worst case scenario has you only out a few bucks. However, when you strike gold (and you will), you will have a new "thing" that you can share with friends. Call that old gang up and get them to meet you at an establishment where one of these bands is performing. Make it a surprise.

Having already scouted ahead, you will know what to expect. Bonus cool points if you go up after the show and "introduce" your friends to the performers. If you stick around after the show that first time, odds are that the band will make an appearance. That is where you do that initial meet-and-greet. Follow them on social media and even share some of your pictures, tagging the band. (I have never found a band to be disappointed with some killer shots of their live performance.)

Most of the guys I have met will be the first to say they are not rock stars. The thing is, that is exactly how the audience DOES see them. I can attest to seeing almost as many females flashing their naughty bits at these events as I did at the big shows. Dudes are still air-guitaring along with the band, and there are a considerable amount of "metal horns" being cast skyward; so, while they might only be filling houses at a fraction of the size of what their namesakes sell, the audience still sees rock stars.

Now is as good of a time as any. I would urge you to set this book aside and perhaps just do a search locally. Start with "Tribute Bands in {insert town here}" and see what comes up. The next step is to just grab your tickets and go. Who knows, by the end of the night you may feel like Marty McFly and Doc Brown...or Mr. Peabody and Sherman.

TRIBUTE

7

Unchained Passion

Every journey begins with that first step. For me, the step that led down the path of my becoming an avid fan of the Tribute Band scene came in September of 2013. The missus was seeking something special for my birthday that year and stumbled across a social media post that announced what was being billed as an "80's Throwback Party" at a small venue called the Hawthorne Theater.

I have always been a music lover. Songs from all genres play throughout my house all day as I work. I believe I have mentioned that I was a regular attendee of the live music scene in Portland, Oregon back in the late 70's and that amazing decade of music…the 80's.

Van Halen (the David Lee Roth era, please) was one of my favorite bands. I still remember staring slack-jawed at my boom box when *Eruption* blared from the speakers that first time. But I digress…

The bands performing that night were all Tribute Bands. The triple-bill would feature a Cult, Poison, and Van Halen Tribute Band. The tickets were around $15!

Seriously? For three bands playing almost four hours of killer rock and roll? How could you go wrong? So, we went to the show. That night, we were actually in the very front, leaning on the stage. I could see the set list taped to the floor which seemed to make the whole thing just a bit cooler.

When the show started, I have to admit that I was not all too familiar with The Cult. I knew the hits such as they were, but after seeing the band Sonic Temple perform, I was more than just a little impressed. However, the next act was Unchained. That is where this love story begins. I wrote a blog post review of the show the following Monday. Little did I know that I was about to follow Alice down a rock-and-roll rabbit hole.

I already shared my review of that show with you as well as the night they performed the entire first album in the order that the tracks appear. I have seen Unchained more than any other Tribute act because I have been lucky enough to form friendships with the members. Lucky me. I want to share my thoughts on their performance at another triple-bill that consisted of them being sand-wiched between Lovedrive (Scorpions) and Crazy Train (Ozzy).

"The middle act was one of my personal favorites: Unchained. I have said it before, and I will say it again. These guys are amazing. They bring you with them on a journey through everything that you loved about the original Van Halen. The big difference is that these guys know you are there and they sin-cerely appreciate their fans...I can tell you that the gang has made some changes. Change is always scary, but when a band does it, they have to try and gauge the crowd to see how it plays out. For Unchained, this change included adding a few "B-Side" songs to their set. As a fan of Van Halen, I was totally thrilled to hear my personal favorite song Take Your Whiskey Home. *The band stepped out on a ledge and, in my opinion, found a bridge to an entire new level of FREAKING AWESOME! There is nothing I can tell you about Unchained that would do the band justice. Don, Brad, Harry, and Dirk will give you a show that will make you remember exactly why you fell in love with this music. They become Dave, Eddie, Michael, and Alex. If you let go for just a moment, you will believe that you have indeed gone back in time and stumbled into something magical."*

I had no idea on that day that I would eventually be calling several of these performers my friends (and not in the verby social media way...nope, these people have actually become real friends over time that I think the world of as people as well as performers).

I remember coming home that night and thinking, *there has to be more of this sort of thing out there.* A quick search and it was like opening up one pre-sent after another. Foreigner, Ozzy, Iron Maiden, Bon Jovi, Journey, Guns N' Roses...and the list went on and on.

Fast forward to when I decided to write about the Tribute Band scene, and the lead singer for Unchained was the first to volunteer, and thus, my first of many interview sessions was conducted. We met up just before he was set to perform another triple bill, this time it would be the aforementioned Motor-breath (Metallica), Lovedrive (The Scorpions), and Unchained (Van Halen) show. Take a moment and let that lineup sort of sink in.

I started by asking this talented and energetic singer (who goes under the name "Donnie Lee" when he fronts Unchained) what he did when he wasn't performing flying splits and immersing himself in the David Lee Roth persona. In other words, what he does in the "real" world.

Donnie Lee (vocals): I'm a complete opposite. I work for The Man…total corporate…insurance. But I get to travel for work and live in hotel rooms, so that provides me with the tour-like attitude, and then I get to play when I come back in town."

Still a neophyte to the scene, one of the things that I had to know was what got him started down this path. I have friends who are musicians, and I'd seen (and played in) my share of basic cover bands; I wanted to know what sent Donnie Lee down the road to being a front man for a full-blown Tribute Band.

Donnie: "Oh, man…I didn't even know I was gonna be in a Tribute {band}. I'd played originals when I was a kid, played in Hollywood…I moved up here and didn't know anybody and said, 'You know, I should probably play music again.' It had been a while, so I did this cover band and this guy comes in to play guitar and tells me, 'I got something else you gotta do.' It was like an 80's overall tribute. Guns N' Roses, Bon Jovi, Dokken and all that. I liked this a lot better and we kinda started dressing up and then the guys in Unchained had a singer and they came to see me play and thought that maybe I might be able to do it. Then I saw *them* play, and I knew I could do that job…I'd love that job. They weren't really yet dressing up and doing the parts. Then they kinda called me and asked if I wanted to give it a shot and I was like, 'Yeah.' Never saw it coming…and then I just sorta ended up here."

The thing about that little story is that it is exactly how so many of the bands I grew up listening to and loving came together. There is a certain chemistry that bubbles to the surface when all the right ingredients are in place.

One of the biggest things about a Tribute Band as opposed to the cover band is the fact that the performers work so hard to recreate the experience of what it was like "back in the day" to see these rock-and-roll legends and icons. A good Tribute Band can transport the audience back in time.

Donnie: "We want to bring back the old classic style of Van Halen so when people come to see it, they say, 'That's what I remember!' A lot of times, the girls do forget that they're not eighteen or twenty-one anymore and we see things that they used to show when they were that age. They forget…they think they are back in the 80's. It's nostalgic…after the first song, the audience might be going 'Hmm…' after the second, 'Okay I kinda get it…' but by the third song they are like, 'Man! Is this Van Halen?' That's the idea. A great example is when I first saw Oliver Stone's movie, The Doors with Val Kilmer as Jim Morrison…first half hour I'm not buying it, but within that next half an hour, I forgot what the real Jim Morrison looked like, and to me, Val Kilmer…that was Jim Morrison. That, to me, is what a Tribute is."

It is difficult enough to keep a marriage of two people together. Things happen. That is the situation that Unchained just went through prior to the release of this book, However, I interviewed Brad "Shreddy Van Halleck" on the same day that I spoke with their front man.

The parting of ways was done with professionalism and the band remains friends with their former member. Their reasons are their own and I did not feel it was any of my business. I did not ask any questions about the reasons behind the new lineup because this is not *that* sort of book. I will let one tidbit of information slip to those of you in the area. Brad…I mean, Dr. Brad Halleck, is a dentist with a very successful practice just across the river in Longview, Washington. How cool would it be to have this guy working on your teeth?

Talking to the Unchained guitarist, I learned the genesis of how the band came together in greater detail. The question was simple; "What got you into the Tribute scene?"

Brad Halleck (guitar): "I was playing in a cover band, just a standard 80's and 90's rock cover band. The drummer in the band had brought the idea of maybe doing a Van Halen Tribute because he knew I liked Van Halen and we played a couple of VH songs…and it kinda lit a little idea in the back of my head. A few years after that, I decided to do it. It kinda sat in the back of my mind for a while until I finally pulled the trigger. What actually made me (pull the trigger) was getting a spot in Crazy Train, the local Ozzy Tribute and about two months into that before we even played a gig I thought 'Why am I not doing my own Tribute? A Van Halen Tribute…we need one in this area.' And so I bailed on that idea and pulled the trigger on doing the Van Halen Tribute. I knew a bass player who looked like Michael Anthony (Harry Bower). And it went through a few different inceptions…it started out just doing a tribute to the music. We didn't dress the part. There was a little bit of push and pull in the band. Two of the members didn't want to do it…the dress-up to fully represent…me and Harry wanted to take it to the next level. I kinda had to make a decision at that point if we could find another singer, and I knew of Donnie Evans. He seemed like he could do this well. He loved the flamboyancy, he totally loves to entertain, and I thought he would be a perfect David Lee Roth. We went through a couple of drummers along the way, but I think we are now a foursome with everybody on the same page."

Much like when a regular part of any ensemble leaves, there is that concern on the side of the fans about whether or not the "new" product can live up to the bar set by what has gone before. The role of Eddie Van Halen would now be picked up by the former guitarist for a band known as Drop Dead Legs who goes by the name of Jim "Top Jimmy" Smoltz.

I was fortunate enough to sit down with the new incarnation of Unchained just days before their unveiling of the revamped lineup and get not only their take on the change, but also be able to listen to their collective ideas; starting with the "Blueprint for Success" as they see it in the Tribute Band scene.

Donnie: "If you're gonna do this, don't do it just to do it or just to be a money maker. You've got to actually be inspired by the music or the part you're gonna play. Don't just do it for a business, because people are gonna see through it."

"Top Jimmy" Smoltz (guitar): "Yeah, along those lines, with the blueprint you're looking for what it is that makes a successful Tribute Band…whoever the public associates with as kinda the "star" of the band or the highlight of the band…those have to be authentic. So whatever the Tribute Band is, whatever that pinnacle is of that actual band, the players have to feel the passion for that position, and they have to BE that position. Otherwise, it's just not successful."

Donnie: "It seems like Jason (Fellman), when we talked about it, said, 'Stop trying to be him, you're not going to fool anybody into believing you are David Lee Roth. You're a natural ham anyways…just do that…but do your best to fill the part, have fun.' You've gotta be having a lot of fun doing it or it's gonna show through."

Harry "Taz" Bower (bass): "I would say that unlike other genres of music, the expectation for accuracy is a little higher. This is a tribute not just to the music, but to the band, so it's a total picture. We're trying to replicate the sound and feel of the CD quality or studio quality. That's what most people want to hear. So first of all, it's learning how to work hard enough to replicate that, and then what is really important is being consistent and giving that same show every single time. Unlike the original act, it's a little bit different. They can change things up; they can be drunk one night…over the years there have been a lot of times where they don't show their best every single concert because they're national icons. Tribute Bands really require work on that accuracy, the energy, the attitude, and, of course, the music."

Dirk Van Nalen (drums): "When I go to see a band I love (or someone copying it) there is a certain way I want to hear it. You know—all those signature licks and such? But, they also gotta be a lot of fun. Guys that just stand there and don't play the part, just wont fly. And I guess I guess if I was going to start a "startup" Tribute Band, Id start an Alice Cooper band. And I get to be Alice Cooper! Every expected signature part would be in place."

Donnie: "Don't half-ass it. Over-exaggerate if you have to."

Smoltz: "You have to be humble about the band that you're trying to be, knowing damn well you'll never be as good as them, but you do your best to try and give the people who are coming to see you the most authentic representation of that band. But you gotta be humble, otherwise you let it go to your head."

Dirk: "We are really just a copy band obviously. Im just so lucky to be able to have fun like this, and people want to see it. Once someone wanted a signed drum stick, and I thought, "Seriously?! I'm not Alex, by any means." It was cool when I was touring with original bands to Europe and such. But, I'm just copying someone."

The conversation naturally turned to the music of Van Halen. If you have never played in a band, you perhaps do not realize that the group assembles a set list which includes the songs and the order they are played. (That would be those little pieces of paper you see getting taped to the floor right before a show. Most bands will happily give them to you after...just don't swipe them BEFORE.)

Donnie: "There is no such thing as a warm-up song. You have to hit 'em in the face right when you come out with a big bang. You have to kind of build a mood...peaks and valleys and then end it on a big bang as well. People come up after the show and tell you how they wanted to go to the bathroom, but they didn't want to leave or they might miss something. You think, "YES!" That's a good set right there."

It is hard to sit down with these performers and not ask them all what they believe the general sense of goodwill that exists between all these bands can be attributed to. Harry Bower had some thoughts on the subject as we wrapped things up.

Bower: "Humble musicians that all have something in common. I'll speak from being a Bostonian for twenty-four years, moving to California for seventeen, and moving up here by choice eleven years ago...it's so much different here. The musicianship, the camaraderie...unbelievable. Part of the reason is that you don't have as many of the bands fighting against one another and competing...we work in synergy here."

8

Jurassic Rock

Every movement has an origin. It is sort of a murky area where many can lay claim to it, some do. In the Tribute scene it might not be possible to say who was first, but it can be said with relative certainty that Rickey Lepinski and Dan Bates are mentioned in that conversation as being part of its infancy.

If you have a moment, set this book down and look up the two on social media. Follow whatever links you have to in order to watch these men perform. The first time that I ever saw Rickey play was during a performance by Maiden Northwest, an Iron Maiden Tribute Band. If you are even a casual fan of Maiden, then you know the bass player, Steve Harris, is perhaps one of the most incredible performers to ever grace the metal stage. Those are some tough shoes to fill, and those were my thoughts as I waited for the band to take the stage.

I have made a lot of friends in the Tribute Band scene these past years, so I don't want to hurt anybody's feelings, but I was blown away by Lepinski's playing and overwhelming stage presence from the first song. Every time since, if he is playing bass in the band, I find myself drawn to watching him perform.

On the exterior, he can look mighty intimidating. The moment that you speak with him, you just know that you are talking to one of the kindest, most compassionate souls you may ever have the pleasure to meet.

His comrade-in-arms is the immensely talented Dan Bates. This is also one of those performers who just looks like he belongs on stage. Whether he is flying through the riffs of Randy Rhodes or effortlessly reproducing the galloping style of Dave Murray, Bates is amazing to watch.

If you are looking for advice from two men that have been around the scene for almost two decades, then look no further. The idea of what a person should consider if they were to travel down the path of starting a Tribute Band might be right here. Point blank, I asked the two what they believed was the blueprint for being successful in the Tribute Band scene.

Rickey Lepinski (bass): "To me, it's really simple. It's your heart and your soul. It's all about your insides and if you are projecting this art from your heart."

Dan Bates (guitar): "I would be more true to the music than the look. It's almost like I would rather see people play in their street clothes rather than wear wigs. If you don't have the look…be true to the music. If you're not a real fan of the music, you probably shouldn't do it. You get a lot of people who do it just because they want to jump on the money bandwagon. If they're not really fans of the (original) band, it kinda comes across that way. Pick a band you love so that, when you're playing it, it doesn't look forced."

Interesting note, it was actually at the Maiden Northwest show that I made the decision to write about the Tribute Scene. This was the show where they brought up a young man who is developmentally challenged (I do hope that is still the correct term, if not, please forgive my ignorance). He was brought up on stage with a guitar and allowed to play *The Trooper* with the band. Now, it was not as if they just brought him up, stuck him off to one side and did the song. Nay, nay, Moosebreath. The band interacted with him like he was just one of the group. They slipped in all those classic 80's era "rock star" poses and made him part of that performance.

Here you have a group of men that are living a bit of a fantasy. For the audience watching, they *become* Iron Maiden. While all of them would blush if you called them rock stars (trust me, they DO NOT consider themselves as such), it bares repeating that this is exactly what they are to those of us in the audience. In that single moment, they let somebody else come in and share in that dream…that fantasy. This is what makes the scene so special. Perhaps Portland, Oregon is an anomaly.

If you are outside this region, maybe you will read a few things you see in these pages and bring them to your scene. Considering the success that Tribute Bands are experiencing here, you may be able to build your own circuit to this level. Just like any journey, the adventure begins with that first step.

The question you may be asking yourself is why would such talented musicians want to make their way playing in a Tribute Band? The choice to do so does not necessarily preclude a person from chasing that dream as an original artist. It simply opens up an avenue to hone the skills it takes to be a performer. When asked, both men had their own unique answer as to why they would/do play in a Tribute Band.

Bates: "It was actually kind of an accident. It just kinda happened. Nobody was really doing it, I mean, by far we weren't the first people doing it. There were other people (groups) like War Pigs and British Steel. It just kinda fell into place. People weren't even really calling them Tribute Bands. It was kinda just a fluke, ya know. Then it took off, and it was seeming to draw a lot of people, so we just kinda kept going."

Lepinski: "I've actually been playing in bands since I was ten years old. I've played original music...nothing but that. I've been down the road, I've had my time in Southern California in the era and heydays of the scene. I was playing it...involved in it, and I did everything that I wanted to do. There was a lot of drugs involved back then {laughs} so not everybody achieved their ultimate goal, but I've been there, and I've done it already. I've thrown my heart out with my music before and I've had it appreciated and I've had it...you know...had my soul ripped out from me when people don't like it...I'm very happy with what I've done in the original music world, and now I love to play live. That's what I *love* to do. I still write music, but I don't put it out there to be judged by anybody just because I do it for the art of it...for an outlet for myself."

Watching Rickey play bass is always a treat. He is a whirlwind of energy from the first note to the last. Dan is up there playing riffs that will make your head spin, but still has time to flash a smile and throw up some metal horns if he sees you aiming a camera at him. Just like athletes, many performers do things to prepare themselves for the upcoming performance.

Lepinski: "I try not to be stressed out, but when you produce the shows—ninety percent of the shows that I play, me and Dan produce—that means you get the date, get the venue, hire everybody else and we put all the cogs together to make the entire event...the day of a show, I try not to be stressed...but Mr. Murphy (of Murphy's Law fame) is always visiting you. If he visits me on my show day, I'm really bitchy...straight up, I try to be as professional as I can, but when show time comes, it all goes away and the energy comes from my heart and my passion for the music itself. If it doesn't come from my heart, I can't act like it, so the energy just wouldn't be there. It's kinda like when we threw together this Foreigner Tribute (Jukebox Heroes), me and Dan Bates, and we thought that we wanted to do it, but it just didn't project from my heart. I didn't necessarily *Want to Know What Love Is* and I didn't really feel that...so we didn't want to fake it...I couldn't fake rock to it."

Bates: "It's a lot of work. It's being there at four o'clock in the afternoon and pretty much staying until the end of the night. The next day is definitely sleeping in until three {laughs} because it is a lot of work. People think, 'Oh, it was a great show. I bet those guys are gonna go party.' You have these people...light men and sound men. You're setting up all afternoon but people don't see that part of it. So the next day is definitely resting...a lot."

Lepinski: "The day after, it's like a buzz. It's almost like a junkie just coming down...I don't know, your ears are just ringing tremendously. You have all the aches and pains that you become addicted to—weirdly. And then the Zen of calm after everything is done and your job has been pulled off and the show has been good. So yeah, just that sense of calm, ear-buzzing pain {big laugh} that I love."

If you are seeking longevity, then maybe heed the words that come from the mouths of two "old school" rockers. Let your passion drive you. Let your love for what you do come front and center stage. Whether you are playing for a roomful of mostly friends and family or in front of a crowd of thousands…live your dream and bring the audience along for the ride.

9

Runnin' Down a Dream

There is just something very cool about Tom Petty. He is that guy that even serious metal heads can listen to and go, "Damn…this dude rocks." His music has become a staple at sporting events, and his popularity has remained solid over the decades.

Sadly, he does not tour as often as fans may like. Fortunately for the people out West, there is Frank Murray. His band, Petty Fever, is an award winning Tribute Band that brings the audience a full Tom Petty experience. His likeness is so amazing, that even close up you would be hard pressed to tell that Frank is not the "real deal".

Murray is no youngster and has probably been involved in music longer than some people in the scene have been alive. Yet, when you see him perform, you would have a rough time pinning an age on the man. His career has brought him a level of success that is enviable.

Frank Murray (guitar/lead vocals): "It kinda goes back years. I've done original bands and had songs on the radio regionally. I've done countless classic rock bands…and some really good ones. It was in the 90's when I had some agents who kept bugging me because I always had that "Tom Petty" look and I kinda have the same vocal range and stage mannerisms, so actually, I didn't have to *try* to do anything. So they kept hounding me for years, 'You gotta do a Tom Petty Tribute.' Back then I worked for an audio products manufacturer called *Carver Pro* and travelled all around the world doing audio trade shows…I just didn't have time to do something like that because I figured that if you are gonna do a tribute to an artist, you better do it right. I don't do anything half-assed."

A musician is like any other artist. Most of them are obsessive about their work. Ask any performer after a gig how they felt they did and they will start picking themselves apart. It is that level of perfectionism that is showcased by Frank Murray and the band, Petty Fever.

Murray: "I was playing with a band, doing all the standard classic rock covers and I'd always end up singing the Tom Petty stuff. I've been a Petty fan since his first show in Portland back in the 70's. Moving forward from there, it was just something on the back burner…I got asked to play at a party and do a bunch of Petty stuff so we put together an eight-song set and played it. It actually went over really well. By then this was the early 2000's."

Perhaps one of the things to take away from this on a personal level is that it might behoove you to take heed of the signs. If you feel a calling, then perhaps you need to answer that call.

So few people truly get to live their dreams because they fear taking that first step. When they do, there is often the feeling of "Why didn't I do this sooner?" If you are lucky to have that calling repeat itself…don't hesitate.

Murray: "When the economy tanked, *Carver* went out of business and I was either gonna get a job at *JBL* in LA or one of the other audio manufacturers. I would have had to move and quit all my bands…so I just sat down and thought about it. I called this one agent that I'd been working on and off with for years who, maybe twelve years prior, had wanted me to do the Petty Tribute. So I asked him if I should still do it and if he could still get me some gigs. He told me to put it together and see how it goes, so I put together a ninety-minute show. I got together with some friends (Tim Baltus, Craig Ostbo, Steve Kuepker, and Jack Codron) that I played with in some classic rock bands over the years. I told them that I wasn't putting together a "bar" band. I was putting together a "show" band and I wanted to do it right, so I made sure everybody did their homework…harmonies, all the parts to make it sound the way it should."

The attention to detail that you will find in the Tribute Band scene is beyond belief. The people that pursue this line of entertainment are very aware of the importance of having the audience feel like they have been treated to some incredible music. If they are able to pull off the look without it becoming a distraction, it adds even greater weight to the performance.

Murray: "We put a show together, the first one in April of 2009 at the Venetian Theater in Hillsboro in front of about 300 people. The place was packed and they just loved us. I'd shot some video at that show and put together a promo and then just made it a full-time job. I can't imagine the time I have put in promoting Petty Fever. There is a lot of "behind the scenes" stuff that people don't realize. I'm on the phone all the time…sending emails…talking to various venues…anybody and everybody."

The part that is often not really considered by the audience is the amount of time spent just getting the act to a stage in front of an audience. Even if they are fortunate enough to have a promoter (like J-Fell Presents) arranging a few shows, most bands still need to arrange their own gigs unless they only want to play two or three times in a year. That is really only a business plan that would work for an act like Pink Floyd. Tribute Bands aren't seeing royalty checks. They live from gig to gig. I think now would be a great time to do a local search and grab tickets to a Tribute Band's show. I will remind you to do this several more times in this book…so get used to it.

Murray: "After that first show…I was just testing the waters. After I felt good about it, I really spent a lot more time studying phrasing on vocals. I didn't really have to study stage mannerisms, it's one of those deals where I just kinda do the same thing he does, so that worked out pretty good. From there it is just a constant learning process. I don't let it go onto auto-pilot. I constantly go back and listen to stuff because it morphs into more of me than Petty after a while. You just kinda have to go back and take a look and a listen."

As is the case with many aspects of the entertainment business. There are awards and accolades to be earned. To the average fan, that might not mean much. As a writer who has never been nominated, much less won anything, I can attest to the fact that it does matter. To be recognized for your work is always something that feels good. Also, it can have a very positive effect on your financial bottom line.

Murray: "After doing this for four years, I got a call from a guy in LA who said that they wanted to nominate me for an award for Tribute Band of the Year. One thing led to another and we ended up winning Tribute Band of the Year at the LA music awards and that opened up a whole bunch of other doors. It's just like…every year things just keep kind of expanding."

If you are seeking success in something, then it only makes sense to get advice from somebody at the top of the game. What better source than an award winning performer who has his own take on the blueprint for making it in the Tribute Band scene. I conclude this chapter with a nugget of advice from somebody who has received some well-deserved accolades for his work in the Tribute Band scene.

Murray: "It's gotta be somebody that is successful…already a marketable product. There are some bands that do tributes to bands that may have had only one or two hits. After that, it is all deep cuts. It's really hard to sell that. After you pick the right artist…do your homework. Study the mannerisms and such. After that, get out there and do the market research and see if people are gonna come see this band. They have to sell the show

TRIBUTE

10

Appetite for Perfection

Later in this book I will be sharing a little bit of insight in regards to what I discovered when asking the members of the various bands that I interviewed which band they would love to play in if their own was off the table. That chapter was almost scrapped when the same answer kept coming up time and again for quite a while.

There is one band that stands head and shoulders above the rest in the eyes of many of their peers. That band is Appetite for Deception. Now, that is not saying that the other bands are not kick-ass and amazing. It simply means that there is one band that has been doing it right for a very long time and their comrades notice.

The scene here in Portland is a bit different than what I expected. I have mentioned that you see a lot of familiar faces in the crowd when attending shows here. And while it is by no means without its own little dramas and squabbles, for the most part, it is very symbiotic. The performers are comfortable enough with their own skills and talents to be able to point out somebody who is doing something exceptional in the realm of Portland, Oregon's Tribute Bands.

When I prepared to write this chapter, I reached out to the band to see if they might be able to give me a few minutes of time for a phone interview. I was invited to attend their rehearsal. That was where I would come to see exactly why this band appeared on season six of **AXS** TV's "*The World's Greatest Tribute Bands*" in early 2016.

I shared just a taste of that experience on my blog the day after that interview was conducted:

"*Wednesday night I was led down a dark corridor to an unassuming door with a massive lock. Nestled away in the Warehouse District of Northwest Port-*

land, I was about to be allowed into the inner sanctum of where The World's Greatest Tribute Band, *Appetite for Deception, hunkers down for rehearsal. One by one, they filtered in. I posted up in a corner feeling like I'd just been given access to the Batcave. And why shouldn't I? After all, this is where five guys gather to transform into their alter-egos. This is where they hammer out the finer points of the numbers they play onstage that come across with a level of perfection that leave fans begging for more.*

*"The night got even better when I was made privy to a song they are working on for future shows. After vowing to keep their secret ("so f***ing cool" is all I kept thinking as I listened to this song being rehearsed), I watched as the members of Appetite fpr Deception discussed certain nuances of the song that needed to be improved in between run-throughs. No matter what direction the suggestion or critique came from, no matter who it was directed at, there were no hard feelings or signs that any of them were unhappy being told where they might not have absolutely nailed it. This is just one reason that this band is the Gold Standard of the Tribute Band scene.*

"My purpose there was to interview this band for my upcoming book, TRIBUTE. I was hoping to throw out a few questions and maybe come away with enough material to assemble a good chapter where this band shares some tips and ideas on how to have a better chance at success in the Tribute Band scene. If I was lucky, maybe a few fun anecdotes about their lives as performers would be thrown my way. By the time I left, I had enough good stuff to do an entire book on just this band. (Who knows...I've already turned one Tribute Band into an evil biker gang rampaging through the zombie apocalypse, you never can tell what I will write next.)

"Besides being amazing hosts and really setting aside some serious quality time for me, they were just an incredible group to talk with. They are all so diverse in their personalities, and through that they have found a way to create magic by utilizing their differences, strengths, and desires."

Something that stood out for me that night was singer Mark Thomas and his absolutely frank and candid attitude. He does not make apologies for his desire to see the band perform with perfection. He has helped to create a culture within the group that its members bring to the other bands that they play with outside of Appetite for Deception.

If you want to see what makes one of the most incredible bands in the scene tick...then settle in as I basically let the members lay out the blueprint for why they can lay claim to being one of *The World's Greatest Tribute Bands.* Let's start with just a simple story of a gig where their "Slash" guitarist was not going to be available to play. They turned to a man they considered to be one of the best guitar players around in Jim "Top Jimmy" Smoltz who was playing with Drop Dead Legs, another area Van Halen Tribute Band. Instead of having him come in and put on the black wig and top hat of Slash, they told him to come in as his Eddie Van Halen character and play the Guns N' Roses music with EVH flair.

Mark "Axl M" Thomas (vocals): "He (Jimmy Smoltz) played with us in 2006 when we were doing a show opening for L.A. Guns and The Bulletboys. It was the first big deal that we had as a Tribute Band opening for some national acts. Brandon (BC Slash) Cook had another commitment in Florida. He was gone, and we didn't want to turn the gig down…so who do we hire…how do we find another Slash at the last minute? Rather than try to find somebody else to wear the hat and step all over our brand we decided that we'd pick the best guitar player in town as Eddie Van Halen to step in. We said, 'Don't be Slash…bring in your striped guitar and learn all the parts…and then you could play *Sweet Child of Mine*, but throw in a little {mimics guitar sounds} and be Eddie Van Halen. I think it was the smartest move we coulda made to find a sub guitar player who was not trying to be Brandon, because you don't need to have confusion about who your guy is."

This would prove to be just the tip of the iceberg with Appetite for Deception. That night, I got the sense that this band was all on the same page. They checked their egos at the door and came together as a single unit to bring the absolute best every single time they take the stage.

To get the information from these guys that a person might want if they decided to start a Tribute Band, I fired off the question: "If somebody walked up to you and asked how they could possibly be successful in the market as a Tribute Band, what advice would you give them?

Brandon "BC Slash" Cook (guitar): "When we put together Appetite (for Deception) eleven years ago, we had the desire to be an arena rock band in a small club. We wanted to bring arena energy…like real huge stage energy to a small venue. We'd all read a bunch of books about groups like KISS and Guns N' Roses and how they created their vibe. We all were on the same page on how we were going to do that. Mark had us watching all the videos of the band live. We started tearing out bits and pieces of their movements…live licks, and stuff like that. It gave me a musical vocabulary to be Slash. The attention to detail is the primary reason to being successful. If you throw those things away and say that it'll be fine without that, pretty much in any band or any business, that's when you start to lose ground because that's when decay starts to happen. You want to have a drive towards excellence. Not perfection, because nothing is going to be perfect. (He described the process all the way down to the top hat of how he built his onstage Slash persona.) It's a lot like acting. If you don't have the intentions to be a bit of an actor, it won't work as well. You must choose to take it that far."

Michael "Izzbo" Killian (guitar): "What it really is, is determining ahead of time that you're going to *be* that band to the best of your capability. There's a lot of bands out there that do really well playing the music. I think we do exceptionally well playing the music, but I don't think that's enough if you're gonna be a Tribute Band. You've gotta do everything you can to be the band...we have weak spots, we have strong spots, but I think the key is to do everything you can for that hour and a half or whatever and remember who the fuck you're working for. You are working for them...for the crowd. You are trying to give them something that they can believe in."

Thomas: "It's deciding which details you are going to choose to ignore. *All* the details are important. You focus on the big ones first...Slash has to have big hair, Slash has to have a hat, Axl has to have a bandana...has to move a certain way. That's where you start. The musicality, of course you do your best and if you're lucky enough to be able to support your character with your ability, you're extremely lucky. Any band out there that says: 'Well, we're just going to play the music and we're not gonna dress the part' sorta becomes one of those gray area bands. It doesn't mean they're not good musicians. It doesn't mean they are not in a "Tribute Band", it just means that they're not putting in the attention the details that we do."

Andrew "Andrew Sorum" Greene (drums): "Different level of show."

Thomas: "(I revealed to the Appetite crew prior to the interview that almost everybody I interviewed when asked who was really doing it right, specifically mentioned Appetite for Deception.) We set our bar where we feel it needs to be and everybody else can either follow our lead or do their own thing. I think that, since our name gets dropped a lot, everybody really respects what we do."

That statement led to a brief conversation about the remarks that I received when I posed the question: *If you could play in any Tribute Band in the local (Portland, Oregon) scene, who would it be?* Time and time again, the response was Appetite for Deception. Their peers see what they are doing and do hold this band in high regard. Brandon "BC Slash" Cook was a leading vote getter amongst his fellow guitarists and is considered to be not simply one of the best...but THE best.

Izzbo: "Just for the record...my position is for sale." {group laughs}

Cook: "Over the last eleven years I've put a ton of time into this position. I've bought like probably five wigs and many replacements for my pants, but that doesn't have anything to do with it."

Thomas: "You gotta quit losing 'em." {more group laughter}

Cook: "Yeah (laughs) you're right...you know, the Slash solos, I want them to be dead-nuts accurate, and Slash is literally one of the greatest guitar players on the planet. You can't walk out there and kinda half-ass them...his style is awesome. He focuses on creating melodies in his solos. There is a very natural flow to them. After learning the notes, I learned how to get into the groove of Slash's solos. Mike pointed out a couple things to me about the groove and that reminded me of the stuff I learned in Jazz school. Put the solos into the pocket that Andrew and Wade are laying down. The vibe of Slash's rhythm playing and solos is very unique, and I put an excessive amount of time woodshedding just that. The Paradise City outro solo was excruciating at first to play live. It's one of the fastest solos in my repertoire. It took a little while to get it where I wanted it because I loved it and respected it as a piece of music that people wanted to hear. Not just any solo, it's so well known."

Izzbo: "If I can interrupt…that is absolutely what you do…but everybody doesn't, and I think that is one of the big things that sets us apart. We're so, you know…anal about being note perfect, and you *kill* that stuff…the point that I'm making is that *you can* walk out there and not nail it, but we chose not to go that way."

Thomas: "There's nothing about our music sonically except for the intricacies that are live…you're not gonna be as impressed with what you hear if you're not there to see it. If you watch it, you're not gonna believe that you're seeing and hearing that at the same time with the nuances of the live performance that we're able to throw in."

This is the Tribute Band idea at its finest. They are fully aware that they are not the actual band, yet they do everything in their power to bring that experience and hazy reality to the audience so that they come away feeling just as happy as if they had seen the real deal. For a group like Appetite for Deception, that allows for some rather odd exceptions when it comes to the lead singer.

Thomas: "The first time we did *Locomotive* live, which was in Richland, and I forgot the lyrics. Lyrically, *Locomotive* is the most complicated song that I'm aware of that Guns N' Roses does, and I could not find a pattern or a method to the lyrics. It was sort of a dry run before we came back to Portland to do it in front of everybody at Harefest (IV). I got through the first verse and I dropped the second verse and I couldn't find my way back in. The band was flawless from start to finish…my vocal in that was shit because I disappeared after the first verse. I went over to the drum riser and I just looked at my five pages…and I have no idea where I am…so I just picked up my drink and I walked around the stage. When something like that happens as Axl Rose, that's the neat thing. I don't think Van Halen could do it, Scorpions can't do it, Bon Jovi can't do it, Foreigner can't do it…you don't have a singer that can totally throw their mic down and walk away. I can do whatever the fuck I want, and it really becomes an Axl Rose moment."

Izzbo: "Yeah, you just have to deal with the band later."

Greene: "He is so in character, once we had an incident where some asshat was trying to burn a flag and he was waving it around, and he got pissed (nods towards Mark), and he just dropped his mic and went to the green room."

Wade "Duff McPoncho" Sardonko (bass): "After screaming at them."

Greene: "We played the rest of the song. People asked us if the whole thing was staged and we were like, 'We weren't sure he was coming back.' He was pissed, but he felt the opportunity and did it."

Appetite for Deception has been around for a while. They have to be considered one of the best in the field now. They play some rather impressive venues, but it was not always that way; we touched on their earlier days for a bit. I asked them what it was like, having played in perhaps smaller clubs and such and now be a featured act at a show like Harefest where they play in front of thousands of screaming fans. Only one member of Appetite for Deception answered, but the nods were universal.

Greene: "To answer the question super concisely…it feels right. In our heads we were already there which I think is why it feels right. We can play a small show in a small place, or a big show with not a lot of people…it is always kind of where we are mentally. A small show, even if it's packed, you just sort of ride off the energy of it, but we still play like we are on a huge stage. But there is always a compromise…when we have room for somebody to run and the drum riser is high enough…all that right stuff for everything to come together, it's how it should be."

Because so many of the members of Appetite for Deception play with other bands, I had to ask them about the symbiotic relationship that seems to be so prevalent in the Portland Tribute Band scene. Most people have this idea that the entertainment business is so cutthroat and self-serving. However, anybody who has been here and attended a few events will start to see that these guys come out for each other on a regular basis. There is a comradeship that is hard to find in entertainment.

Izzbo: "I got something to say about that, but I don't have an answer for your exact question, but what I can say is that in this town…this is where I've been for most of my performing life, it didn't use to be this way. It was just as cutthroat as anyplace you can imagine. In the 80's and early 90's it was very competitive, very like that 'high school' kind of band rivalry. Tearing people's flyers down, putting yours up. But it just isn't (like that) now, and I'm happy it's like that…it's a lot cooler and really makes a better scene, I think, for everybody because the big reason why is that you're not asking your fans to choose sides."

Thomas: "You didn't answer his question." {laughs}

Izzbo: "I know…I said I wasn't gonna from the get go…shut up!" {more laughter}

Greene: "The answer honestly is Jason (Fellman). Not completely, but in part. And…everyone's a little older than when you are clawing to make it when you're twenty."

Thomas: "We're not in our twenties…that's a big part of it."

Greene: "But you've got this thing in Jason, kind of a 'no bullshit' guy, and, however his business theory works, he's always honest with you. Because of that, and because of his ethics with money in stuff, the best people in town sort of end up in that circle. All that is happening is really positive, so when someone comes in or a band comes in and they're not…it sticks out that much more. It's really, really easy to spot someone whose attitude doesn't fit. I think even Don (Evans) was talking about that when he was new. It was shocking to him that it was actually real and sincere that people were that nice. I think he said something about it taking him a while to relax in it and really trust and embrace it."

Thomas: "There are other Tributes in town that are not part of this circle and you really just don't hear that much about them. There are a few that if I really thought about it, I could probably list four or five. But I have no idea when they ever play or where."

Greene: "It's like what you were talking about with the symbiotic situation, because there is competition, I mean, don't fool yourself. But if every band is sort of friendly rivalrying and upping their game, and all the bands are good, then that decreases the risk from a fan perspective that you're gonna get a show that sucks. So, if you trust in the scene more, you're more willing to take a chance or go to a place you haven't been to or see a band you haven't watched. So really, us cooperating is an unintended side-effect where we are all better, we're all paying attention to what we're doing and the whole Tribute scene at least is sort of elevated by that."

Thomas: "Nobody wants to see Guns N' Roses play every weekend. But if you can see Heart play, and Zeppelin play, and Foreigner, Guns N' Roses, Bon Jovi, Scorpions, Ozzy, and Maiden play, and every week you've got somebody that you grew up with that will take you back in time to 1982, '85, '87, '91…you can see it all, and it's all gonna be good. And then you're ready to go back to the beginning of the cycle again and see whatever that band was that you saw initially. That gives us all a means of keeping this wheel going."

Some of what did not make these pages were the friendly jabs and some of the banter that took place. Obviously it would not make sense to transcribe the entire interview. As it started to wind down, I was able to let these guys know how those of us in the audience see them. It might strike you as funny, but these guys don't see themselves as rock stars. They all feel blessed to do what they do, but at the end of the day (and this is a sentiment that I got across the board as I interviewed band after band), they are just doing something they enjoy. It just so happens that it is performing on stage. That prompted the next exchange. This, I believe, is why Appetite for Deception is perhaps *The World'sGgreatest*

Tribute Band...and they don't need a television show to allow them to stake that claim.

Greene: "For us, I think it's not playing a part. I've internalized a lot of it."

Thomas: "You get through that first song, and I think you really have to become your character, especially once we start hitting the ballads. In order for the ballad to make sense to the crowd...I really start to feel the songs and have to sometimes pull myself back from the emotional part."

(Of course this prompted more good-natured chiding from the band as Mark revealed the true emotional side of his immersion into the role he plays on stage.)

Thomas: "You can feel it. I mean, I didn't write the songs, but I'm singing them. Singing gives you a different kind of connection to the lyrics that's in there. If you're playing and you're listening, and playing your part, you might also find the same thing. I've read everybody's books that are out there: Steven Adler's, Duff McKagan's, Slash's, several of them by Axl...I've read 'em all, so I kind of understand part of the history...when I sing some of the songs, I have my own interpretation of what I believe they meant when they were being written. The ballads, sometimes you personalize them. This is why the songs are so important to the listener who saw the video *Patience* for the first time in 1989, and it meant something to them when they saw it. Well, we have those feelings too. We watched MTV growing up, so we have our own feelings for what the song meant. Couple that with what you think the artist...what Axl might have meant when he wrote it, or Izzy might have meant when he wrote it and you can get kind of lost in that sense and you have to pull yourself back from it. You have to pull back from yourself and get back into your character and what your character would do on stage...if it's genuine emotion, the audience can feel it. They know. Whether your sad because you're singing *Patience*, or your singing *Coma* which is this really tumultuous thing with a drug overdose and 'I don't wanna live anymore'...I've broken stages with my mic stand swinging it and broken holes in the stage and the crowd loves that. I like it...when I do it, it's this giant release."

Greene: "We've all gotten overboard where you let the intensity carry you away...I think I did that and I got pissed and I threw a stick."

(This statement prompted the band to offer up a variety of bloody results including lost eyeballs and other equally gruesome outcomes.)

Cook: "When I first got to do this, I always wanted to be able to do what Slash did on stage...he'll run like mid-solo across the stage and jump. He (nodding to Mark Thomas) brought this training thing on stage like a lion trainer thing (Mark identified it as a plyo-box). I jumped off of it and went five feet in the air, I don't even know how high I got. I landed and I lost my balance and went 'BAM!' right into the wall. And in Sioux Falls, South Dakota I jumped in the middle of the stage and I fell flat on my back...there is nothing that can replace that with this band...going a hundred miles per hour every show until the end note where you're just seething. I figured if I was going to put on a GnR show it had to be nearly falling apart at all times. Falling a few times was kind of part of the deal."

I do want to take just a second to acknowledge the bass player (Wade "Duff McPoncho) Sardonko. While he does not show up much in what you read here, he was regularly part of the banter that took place between band members over the course of our interview. Like many bass players I have met, he seemed content to agree with much of what was said and just sort of chilled out as he listened. He was not left off because he did not have anything to say, he was simply a man of few words and a lot of expression.

Appetite for Deception is regularly referred to by their fellow Tribute comrades as a benchmark for how to do it right. They are unapologetic about their attention to detail and believe that the methods they have crafted to turn their band into such a success are helping in the other bands they perform with as well as their "regular" lives. There was one poignant exchange that really shows the grasp that this band has in regards to who they are in the music world.

Thomas: "When we played at the Knitting Factory in Spokane and we pulled up along the street...I looked at the marquee and it said 'Appetite for Deception'. When you look at that in the eyes of somebody that has no idea what that means...you've just lost. It should say 'Guns N' Roses Tribute...Appetite for Deception'."

Cook: "Yeah, absolutely."

Thomas: "Because, Guns N' Roses is what people want to see. That's the product that we deliver. Our name is Appetite for Deception. And we hope that, after somebody's seen our show, they will follow us...and appreciate the authenticity that we brought to it. This is not something that we've created. It is not something that we get royalties from. Every Tribute out there should spend less time talking about their own name, and more time talking about the name that they're portraying out there, because that's the money. People are reminiscing where they were back in, you know, 1980 to 1990-whatever-the-Tribute Scene-is. That's where the money is."

Greene: "We're selling to a degree...nostalgia. Our industry is nostalgia."

I walked out of that interview firmly believing that I could write an entire book on them alone...and maybe, in the future, I will.

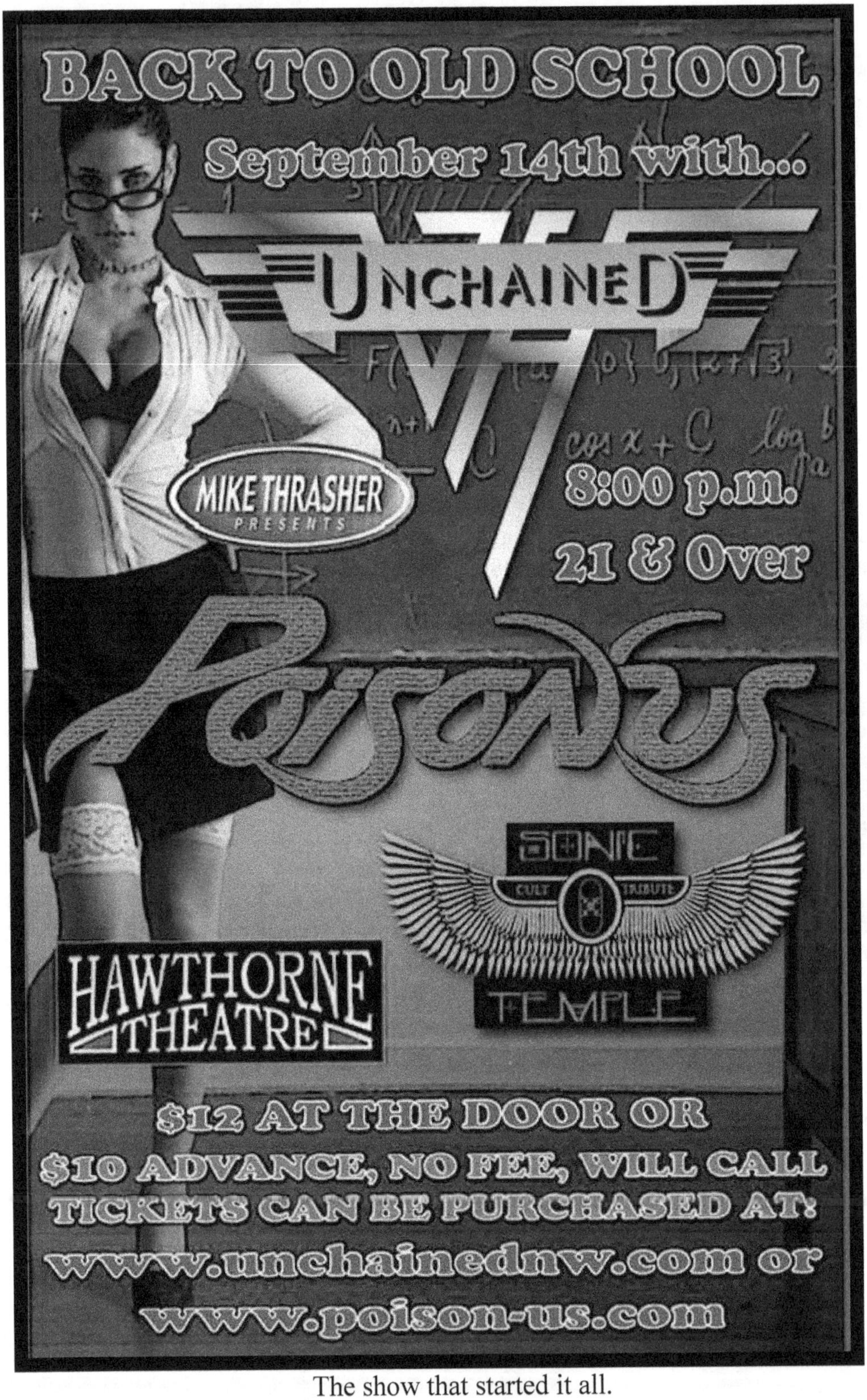

The show that started it all.

Unchained's Donnie Lee as David Lee Roth

Unchained's Harry 'Taz' Bower and Diamond Donnie Lee

Appetite for Deception's Mark Thomas as Axl Rose

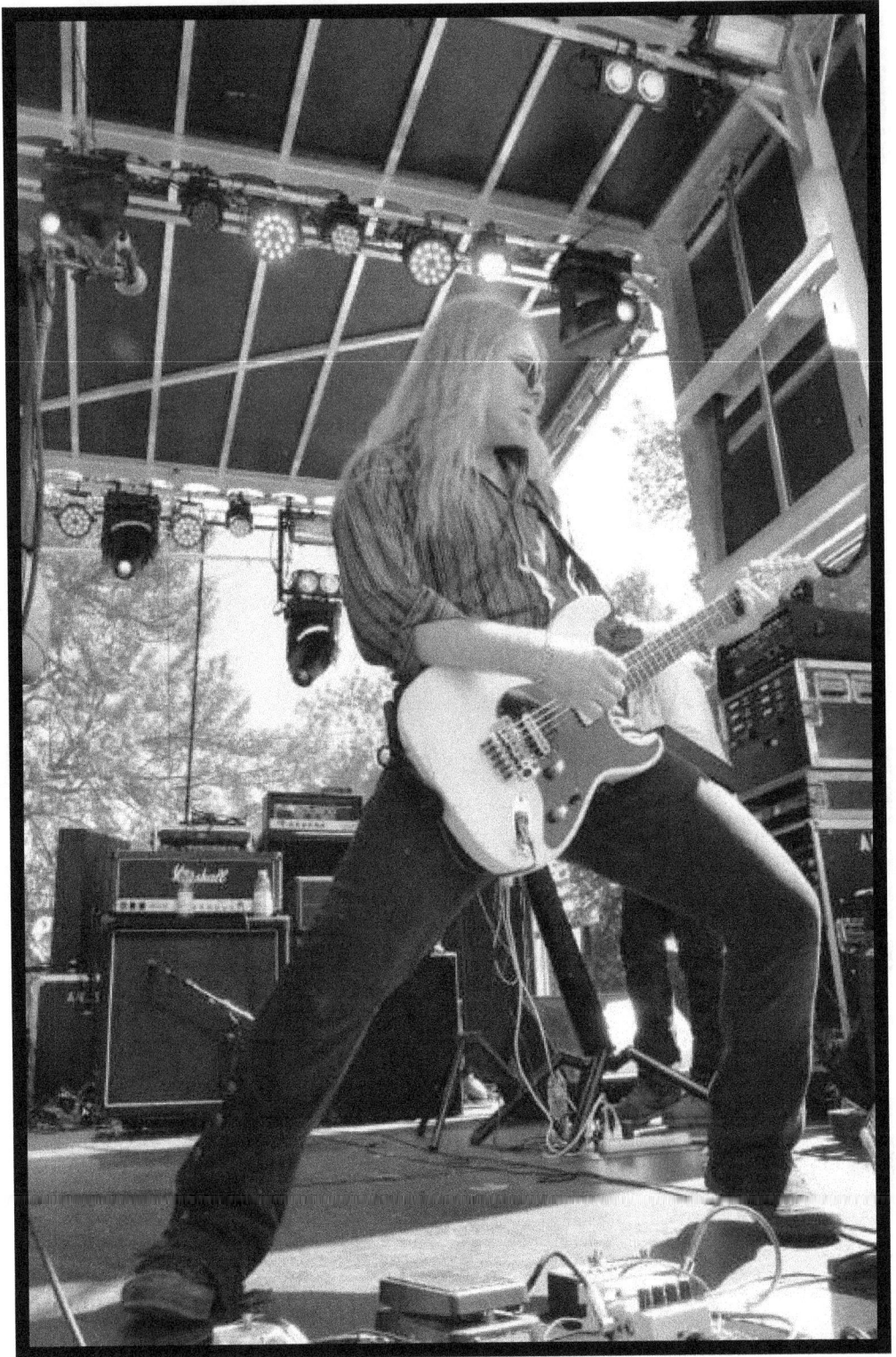

Juke Box Heroes' Brandon Cook

Petty Fever's Frank Murray

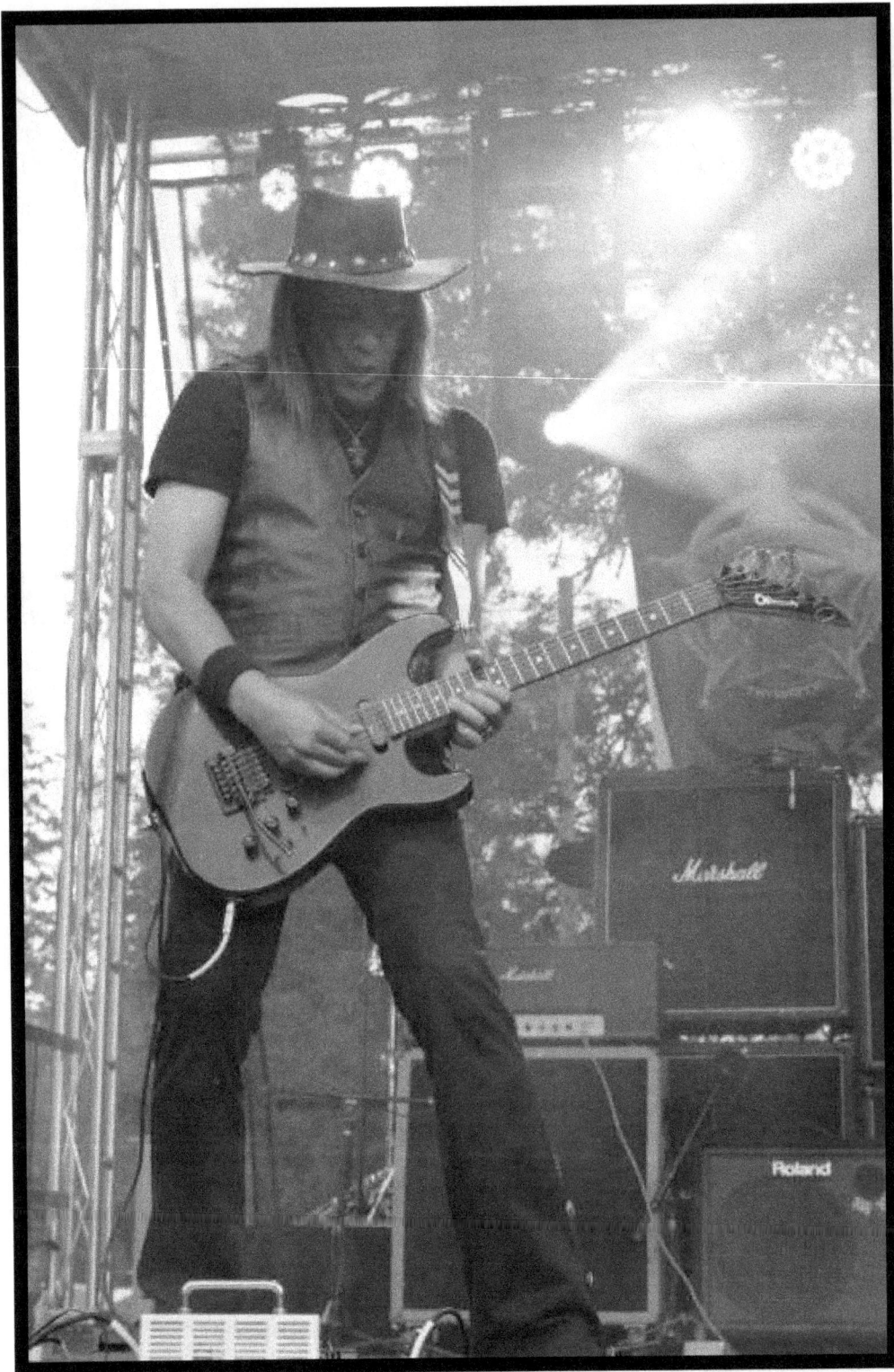

Steelhorse's Brian McGroovy as Richie Sambora

Grand Royale as the Beastie Boys

Lovedrive's Larry Smith belts out the Scorpions

Motorbreath's Joe Spencer is a show stopper on drums

Motorbreath's frontman Kevin Staley

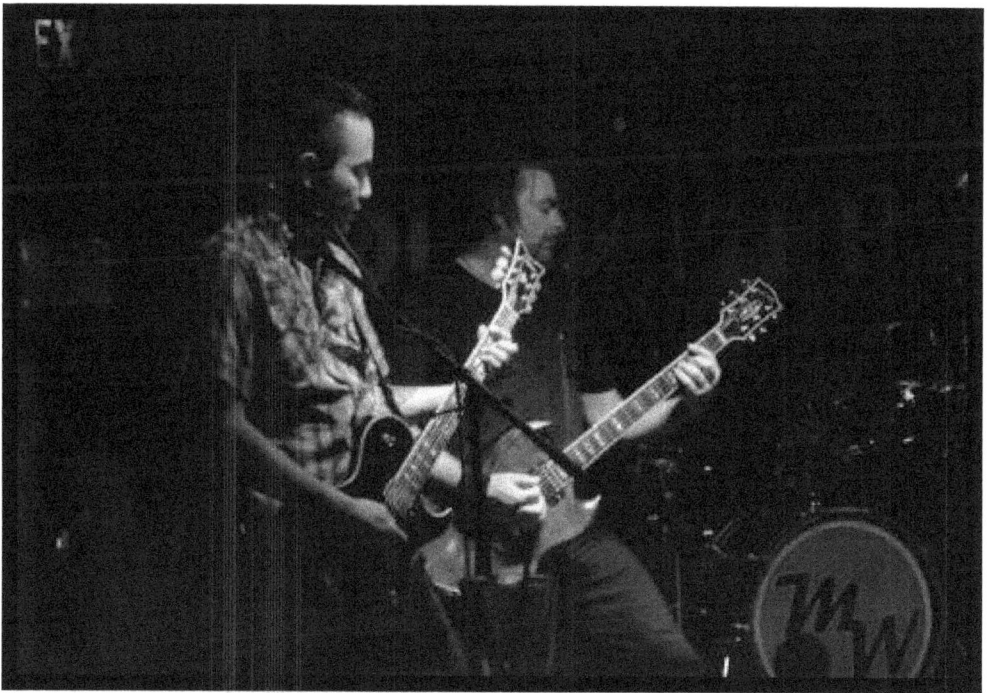

Monkey Wrench tackles the Foo Fighters

Poison'us frontman Will Barnes rocks the house as Brett Michaels

Lovedrive stings the Scorpions

Appetite for Deception AKA The World's Greatest Tribute Band

Ramble On's Rich Ray…

Ramble On's Steven Adams with the classic Jimmy Page doubleneck.

Stone in Love's Kevin Hahn

Shoot to Thrill rocks AC/DC

Barracuda's DL Car is Almost Ann of Heart

Poison'us locks in their sound

Steelhorse's Kevin Rankin

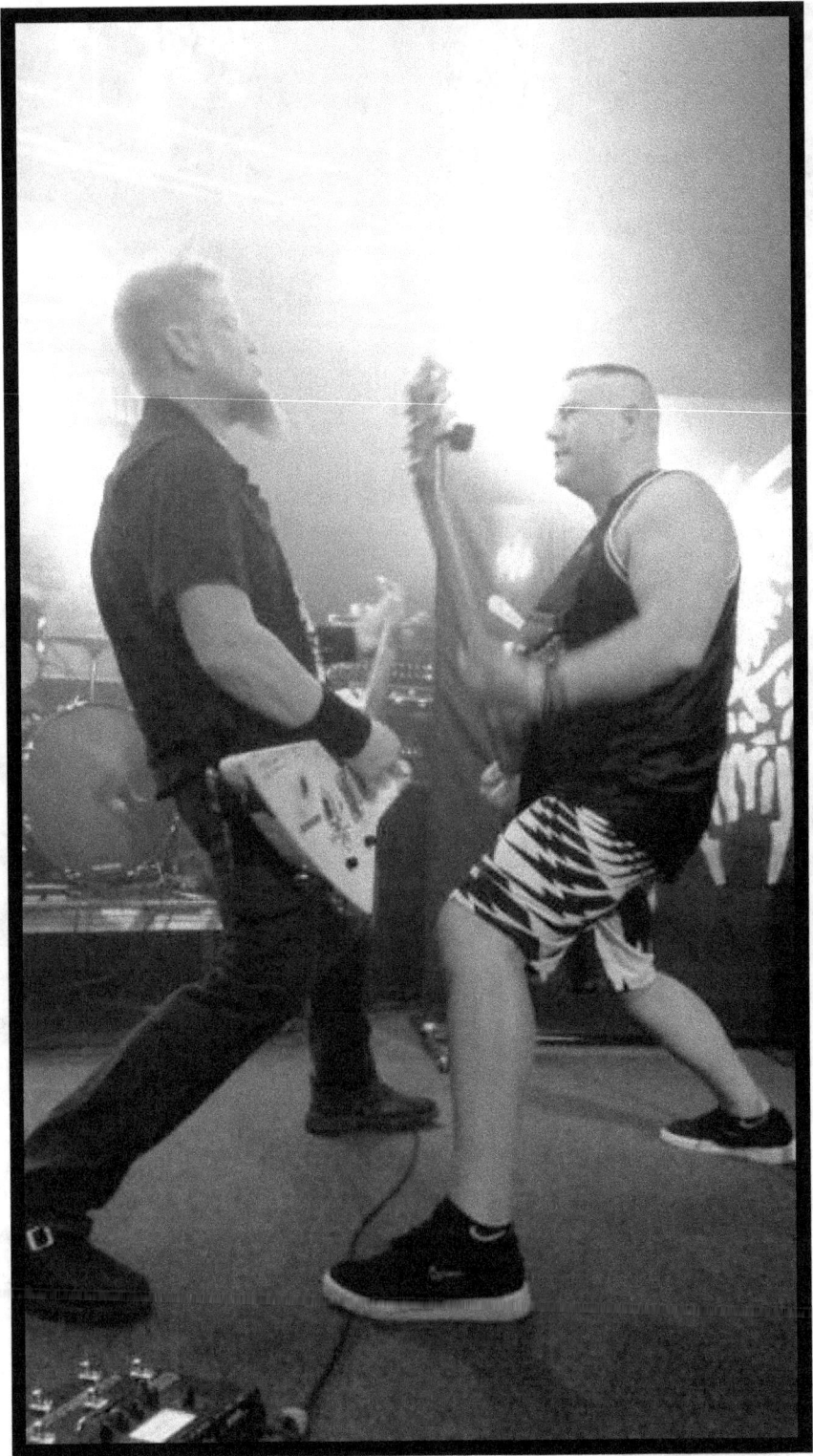

Motorbreath plays some serious Metallica

Motorbreath's Bob Capka

The Ambassador of Good Times…Jason Fellman

Maiden Northwest's bass player Rickey Lepinski

Unchained's 'Top Jimmy' Schmoltz

Monsters of Rock…Dan Bates and Rickey Lepinski

Steelhorse's Mark Thomas as Jon Bon Jovi

Same Ol' Situation's Jon Abell as Nikki Sixx

Thank you!

Goodnight!

11

The Crown Jewel

Back in the 80's there were so many amazing outdoor stadium shows featuring the biggest bands on these five and six (or more) group super shows. There is a small town outside of Portland, Oregon called Canby. Unless you are local, chances are you have never heard of it. Yet, every summer for the past several years there has been a music event known as Harefest that hearkens back to those outdoor mega-events.

In 2016 there are sixteen bands playing over a two-day period. The lineup is basically the "who's who" of the local Tribute Band scene. It had to change venues recently because it had pretty much outgrown its old home. For less than the price of a "cheap seat" at a concert featuring acts that may or may not have the original members that you grew up listening to, you are treated to two days and nights of some amazing rock and roll.

This is the show that bands yearn to perform at. It is a chance to get out in front of three thousand-plus people and put on the show of a lifetime.

Harefest V was a special thrill for me because I was given full press access by Jason Fellman of J-Fell Presents. During the two days of the event, I shot close to a thousand pictures. (It doesn't matter if only about five hundred were useable; I'm a writer not a photographer!) This is what I had to say about that two-day music extravaganza. The headline asked the simple question: Was it really that good?

"Yes! The answer is an emphatic "YES!" This past weekend, J-Fell Presents and the overwhelming talent that Jason Fellman has assembled put on an epic performance. This year, Harefest V must be considered the premiere concert event of the year; not just locally, but nationwide.

"Where else could you see thirteen bands ranging from Heart to Metallica over a two-day period, and pay less than a hundred and fifty bucks for not one,

but two people to attend? That was the case as over three thousand people per day converged on Pat's Acres in Canby, Oregon (the new venue replacing the back lot of the Wild Hare Saloon due to such a large crowd) to be rocked long and hard.

"Okay, so the "real" bands were not in attendance, but if you have checked the lineups in most of the bands that I am about to talk about (in their Tribute form), you will see that they often lack all of their original members. Additionally, Tribute bands really do try harder. As a long time attendee of the concert scene starting back in the 70's, I have seen some VERY disappointing and lackluster performances from the actual bands. What makes the Tribute scene so amazing is that these people truly love what they do, and they are genuinely appreciative of the people who come to see them play. Ask yourself this, how many times have you sipped a beverage and talked about what you just saw with the members of Van Halen?

"Oh, I imagine you could purchase some special package ticket deal and the band would zip past you in some reception room. But at pretty much every show that I have attended in the Tribute scene, I have had the pleasure of meeting many of the band members and actually having normal conversations.

"But, back to the show. Day one kicked off with the Unchained boys coming on strong with perhaps the best Van Halen Tribute look, sound, and feel (basically all the good stuff from the 80's Van Halen heyday minus DLR forgetting the words or stumbling around in a drunken stupor). Brad "Shreddy Van Halen" Halleck wins the "Best Smile" award as he becomes the guitar legend from my youth. The entire band put on an excellent show and got the crowd primed for what was to be a night of the "hard stuff". The easiest way to describe an Unchained show is a party for your ears that leaves you feeling good, but wanting just a bit more.

"Lovedrive wins the "Lazarus Award". This is a Scorpions Tribute band that vanished from the scene for a few years, but has come back stronger than ever and are not afraid to pull out the deep tracks that will have you rushing home after and pulling out your old Scorps collection and skipping all the hits just to hear those amazing non-radio songs that the band pumped out. Additionally, when they take the stage, you are almost positive that Klaus Meine is up there belting out the tunes. Vocally, this is a band that is an example of perfection. Toss in the fact that they absolutely shred their set with an obvious love of their material, and Lovedrive is a band to add to your "Must See" list. From start to finish, they had the crowd in a frenzy.

"Crazy Train followed with Tim Tugg allowing the spirit of Ozzy to take over his body for an hour. This is a band with perhaps the most amazing bass player on the Tribute scene in Rickey Lepinski. They took the stage as darkness fell, and it was fitting as their sound seeped into the night and drew the crowd

closer to the stage. The spot on sound of these guys was a treat as always with Dan Bates putting forth some of the slickest guitar work that two hands can manage. Simply put, these guys are a highlight reel from start to finish.

"If you ask the members of many of the other Tribute bands, they will tell you that Appetite for Deception is the best there is on the scene. They have the look and feel of the classic G-n-R band that took the music world by storm back in the 80's. For me, Guns-and-Roses is one of those bands that I have an "I remember where I was" when I first heard them. I was not disappointed. Appetite for Deception took me back to some great memories with their set. If I had to make any critique, it would be the choice of their closing number. The song was spot on, but just seemed like an odd way to end (unless you understand the antics of their namesake). However, in keeping with the G-n-R attitude, I would not be surprised if that is by design. This band has the walk-off down perfect as the song ends and they just leave. Naturally...the audience wants more.

"That would bring us to Motorbreath. These guys bring on some serious Metallica chops with a drummer in Joe Spencer that should get together with Lepinski and see which one runs out of energy first. Seriously, the drum-and-bass engine of this motor is eight cylinders of serious metal with Mark Trees as the massive bass monster from Hell. With Kevin Staley as the growling front man and Bob Capka on guitar, the audience was given something stronger than any coffee to keep them awake into the wee hours of the morning. Nobody can say that they did not get more than their money's worth after day one...but that is the thing; it was ONLY DAY ONE!

"Day two was a scorcher and the sun had many fans seeking a number of ways to cool off. Any area that provided shade was elbow-to-elbow as all but the most stalwart rock fans braved the heat when day two opened with Jukebox Heroes.

"With this being my first time seeing this Foreigner Tribute Band, I was not only impressed with the vocals, but for me, the highlight was the killer saxophone player! I could rave about how they took on all the hits with ease and sounded great (I was hoping for Starrider, but maybe finding a flute player as good as their sax man was too tall of an order. Note to Band: The lead singer from Barracuda plays flute. Just making a request.)

"The sounds of Foreigner proved to be an excellent way to get the day rolling. And this band does not disappoint. As with the other bands, these guys came out to the crowd after their fantastic set and posed for pictures as well as mingling. What made that even more impressive was the fact that front man Rich Ray would be returning to the stage with Zeppelin Tribute, Ramble On in just over an hour.

"Keeping the mellow vibe, while still kicking it up a notch, the award winning Tribute band, Petty Fever gave the heat something to compete with. This *would make two bands in a row that I would be seeing for the first time. Kudos to Jason Fellman for having such an eye for talent. Frank Murray is not only a visual ringer for 70's, 80's, and 90's rock icon Tom Petty, but his vocals were crystal.*

"The shadows were growing longer, but it was still scorching on stage with Ramble On taking the crowd back to the days when Led Zeppelin cranked from every 8-Track player up and down the strip. This is one of those bands that can be tricky. There is a musicality to Zeppelin that hides under the crunch. Ramble On obviously understands this fact.

"Barracuda, the Heart Tribute Band, is another band that makes you feel as if you stepped into a time machine. This band was also one of the most diffi-cult when it came to choosing a picture to share. They hold the distinction of being the only female act at Harefest V. (Jason, I beg you, scour the globe for a Joan Jett act!) These ladies are just so amazing. Vocally, Donna Caruk is so damn good that you will fall in love with Heart all over again. They put on a spectacular show and were the perfect bridge from day to evening.

"With the sun down, it was time for Steelhorse, the Bon Jovi Tribute Band. This is a group that has become my "dirty little secret". Honestly, back in their prime, I was not a Bon Jovi fan. Probably because Jon Bon Jovi is so damn pretty. Mark Thomas could be JBJ's twin. Not only that, but I think he has mag-ic powers, because he converted me into a fan last year at Harefest IV when I saw him for the first time. It was more of the same this year as the band cast their web over the crowd and owned the stage. This is a Tribute band at its best. I say that because these guys have that look and feel. They exude "Rock Star" the entire time they are on stage.

"What can be said about Journey Tribute Band Stone in Love that has not been said? They are superb, and that rests on the shoulders of the super-talented Kevin Hahn, but is amplified by the deceptive harmonies that take place vocally underneath Hahn's Perry-esque range. This band came out with what could very well be the show closing performance despite there being two bands remaining. Hit after hit came and the band took full advantage of a light show that made the entire venue glow with pinks and purples. The best way to describe their set? WOW!

"The penultimate band of the night was relative newcomer, Grand Royale. This Beastie Boys Tribute Band was actually the act I was most excited to see. Having caught them at another venue a couple of months ago, I felt like my up-petite had barely begun to be satisfied. I was in luck at Harefest V with a set from three bad boys you know so well. They absolutely did not disappoint. If I did not mention their band, The White Castle Crew, I would be remiss. I still do not know the name of the bass player, but he brings some serious funk to the set. When they said goodnight, it left one more band...

"Shoot to Thrill would put the exclamation point on two days' worth of some amazing music. This is AC/DC with the volume turned up to 12. The look is there, and if you ever witnessed Angus and his trademark leg-and-head bounce as he strutted and hopped around the stage, then you can appreciate the work that Shoot to Thrill puts in to reproduce the experience.

"When it was over, I did not hear one person complain. Perhaps that was due to my hearing not being as sharp as it had been forty-eight hours prior...or maybe J-Fell Presents and the Wild Hare Saloon actually managed to come together and create the ultimate outdoor music festival. Yeah...I am betting it was the latter. This event offered the biggest bang for your buck and sent a total of around 6,000 people out those gates over two nights combined with some memories that will last forever. Along the way, a lot of people are now able to say, "Hey! This weekend I met the (singer, guitarist, drummer, etc.) of this band that YOU have to see next time they play."

Going into the 2016 edition, Unchained is set to make their third appearance. They have been one of the earlier acts in years past. It is not lost on bass player Harry "Taz" Bower the honor and importance of taking the stage after dark when the crowd is at its peak and the lights are at their brightest. When the subject came up, you could hear the smile in his voice.

Harry Bower (Unchained): "This is the best natural high ever. It's why I do this. I can't speak for others, but you don't get necessarily rich monetarily by doing this. But you do get rich being able to exchange the energy with the crowd. The larger the crowd, the more energy. It's the pinnacle of why we do it. I will speak for our band, we play straight, and the high you get off of playing for ninety minutes non-stop with high energy rock-and-roll, there's nothing like it. In the case of our band, we try to listen to the audience, and I think we've done that by nature of what Van Halen does with their style of swing-rock music."

Harefest is something to behold. Every band that lands a spot knows that there will be a massive crowd. They know that expectations are high all the way across the board. This is the show when nothing can be held in reserve. The size of the crowd is not lost on them, and all of the bands selected to perform go into, and come away with, what has to be considered a "lifetime" experience.

Maury Brown (Shoot to Thrill): "It's just too much fun seeing that many people having fun. To be part of that is just really exhilarating...it's just been a joy to do it (Harefest). The fans are fantastic. I can't emphasize that enough. The people that come out and witness this whole thing, you know, I always sit there and joke 'They do realize that we *aren't* AC/DC, right?' The fans are into it...they really absorb it like they're at a show of the bands that we tribute, and I think that is a testament to the bands...to Jason (Fellman), and all the organizers. It's a quality live performance that rivals many bands that come to town that are national acts. Before Harefest, we'll probably have four or five (re-hearsals). We really just kind of go over the continuity of things and how we're going to choreograph stuff. We shake the set list up and do the production element. We try to make our show fresh every Harefest. Every time you come to see us at Harefest, it's our desire to have something exciting and new in terms of production that you haven't seen before."

Steve Adams (Ramble On): "One time, I actually saw a woman weeping. I've never really seen anybody cry. This person was moved by the music. She was watching the band in tears. That was pretty incredible to witness. Apart from that…watching people just scream…their hands raised…with absolute attention to what you're doing. That is some of the best. The people up front that I can literally see…you can't really see much past twenty feet beyond the stage…but in that range, that's what I see. Faces with adulation, with perfect attention and joy. I come up close to the edge of the stage and I've had people try to touch me like I'm a bloody rock star (laughs) and its…that's just amazing to see and to feel."

During my time interviewing the band Appetite for Deception, I had the interview tables turned on me by lead singer Mark "Axl M" Thomas. At Harefest V, they ended their set with what many non-Guns N' Roses fans would consider a bit of a B-cut song. They finished the number and then just walked off the stage.

For those of you not familiar with the actual live performances of GNR, that is exactly the sort of thing that the band does. That last song by Appetite for Deception was a calculated risk; to end on a song that was not a huge hit was not unanimously liked by all band members. It was eventually agreed upon, and that night at Harefest, it was put into play.

As a fan of the original band, I saw the situation for what it was and when people around me started asking when they were gonna come back on and finish…I knew it was not going to happen. Appetite had sunk deep into their roles in order to further the illusion.

Mark Thomas (Appetite for Deception/Steelhorse): "So what is your honest opinion last year (at Harefest V) of our set?" (He hushed the band and leaned forward with just a hint of a gleam in his eyes.)

Me: "I will say that when you guys finished, I could not believe you were done. Then I looked at my wife and said, 'They did just what Guns N' Roses would do. They played a B-cut and then walked off.'"

(*Author's Note: I will say that I like GNR. They are not my favorite and I don't maybe obsess over them like I might with KISS, Aerosmith, or Van Halen, but I do dig their music. I will play an entire GNR album on a rare occasion, but I have their biggest hits on my portable music device. They ended with the song* Estranged *from* Use Your Illusion II. *Did the song have a video and get some play? Sure, but it was simply not one that jumped out at me like* You Could Be Mine, *or* Civil War.)

Thomas: "It's not easy to agree upon how a set is gonna work out. I'm extremely passionate about the direction of everything and I have to twist a lot of arms to make things happen and not everybody is happy about the way it works out...or agrees that it's right, and it isn't always right. You got it. Let's say there are only a dozen people there that got it. That makes me happy. Now that may not make everybody else in the band happy, but I believe that it makes the point of what we're doing and that kind of turmoil really drives the rest of the bands in town to try to do something unique. If we can leave people with a little bit of angst, wondering, 'What the fuck was that?' I don't really care. We play something that showcases our musical ability, our sense of timing, our ability to reproduce note-for-note everything in a ballad like *Estranged*...it's an epic ballad."

Brandon Cook (Appetite for Deception/Jukebox Heroes): "It's also a video. It shouldn't be considered a B-cut. But people don't really know it anymore. It's a great song...classic. I wish we could get away with the deep cuts sometimes."

Thomas: "But it's not a radio played song because it's ten minutes long. There were a lot of people that asked me, 'What was that?' because they didn't know the song...it's a really good feeling to walk away, we scratch our own heads and pat our own backs and go, "Oh, my God, that was awesome! That felt so good (long pause) was that a good idea?'" {band laughs}

Harefest is also a great place to bump into the performers. Just like you, they are often out in the front of the stage taking in the music. You never know who you will bump into while waiting in line for a frosty, cold beverage.

Brian McGroovy (Steelhorse): "Harefest...I would still call that an intimate setting...even though there are a few thousand people there. It's still an intimate setting that you can go out there and just mingle, for lack of a better term. Stand out there and enjoy the other bands that are playing. And if somebody comes up to you and says, 'Hey, I caught your show. It was really awesome!' You thank them and tell them you are glad they had a good time. Then you might discover that they are super huge fans of that music, and tell you how much they appreciate it. And you know, you just kind of give it back to them. I've provided one part of the party, now I want to have the rest of the night with what they had."

TRIBUTE

12

It ain't all Glam

While it is apparently slanted towards acts that dominated the 80' there is a surge of some good 90's music starting to work itself into the Tribute Band arena. The "Grunge" era was ushered in by groups like Nirvana, Pearl Jam, Alice in Chains, and Soundgarden. While they are often thought of as wearing mostly flannel, these acts were simply abandoning the glitz and flash that had dominated the 80's.

Also gone were the blazing guitar solos. While there was an amazing degree of musicality shown by many of these acts, there was nothing that took center stage like the Eddie Van Halen or Randy Rhodes type of shredding solos that the "Hair" bands had built around over the past decade.

People wanting to carve out a place for themselves by playing the 90's era rock were going to have to face a different set of obstacles. One of the acts up to that challenge is Monkey Wrench (Foo Fighters).

Seeing them live, I will simply state that they impressed the hell out of me. This is what I had to say in my review of their show in June of 2016:

"Saturday night, the wife and I did something we simply DO NOT make a habit of doing. We went out. It wasn't the going out part, but the fact that we LEFT our house at 9:30 to drive an hour to see a band we had never seen play live before. The band in question was Monkey Wrench—a Foo Fighters Tribute Band. If you are going to catch a band like Monkey Wrench for the first time, then a "no frills" location like Dublin Pub is the perfect location. As I said, Monkey Wrench is a Foo Fighters Tribute Band. Now, let me just say that I have seen others (Foo Fighters Tribute Bands). I will go on record as saying that Monkey Wrench is THE Portland, Oregon area Foo Fighters Tribute Band. Let me also add that I believe you will hear a lot more about this band over the coming months.

TRIBUTE

"So, let's get the critique part of this out of the way. This band has only one handicap that I can think of right off the bat: Song Depth. I am not saying they can't fill a set. They absolutely can and did the other night. The only drawback is that, if you are not a Foo Fighters fan, then there will be about a third of the songs in the set that you won't know due to lack of radio play. This negative is turned into a positive by the MW crew due to the energy of their performance. Sunday, I had to dial up a few songs from their set list and listen to them as per-formed by Dave Grohl and the True Foo. One song in particular is Walk. *The drumming alone will cause you to fall in love with this tune. Christian Smith gives a performance that captivated Denise in a way that, so far, only Joe Spencer of Motorbreath has accomplished.*

"This could signal a renewed surge of 90's bands sliding into shows around Portland. There are a few, but if more bands put in the work like Mon-key Wrench, alt-rock fans may find themselves experiencing a state of Nirvana. (See what I did there?) This is a show that does not pull any punches, and by the end, you have to wonder how front man Jon Johnson is able to speak.

"That brings me to the important part of this review. Yes, they play ALL the FF hits. There may only be 8-10 that you recall from the radio, but don't be surprised if you discover a few new tunes that make their way onto your music device's playlist.

"Johnson does a decent job of pulling of the 2003 look of Grohl with his straight locks hanging down in his eyes. He obviously works at the physical mannerisms I remember from seeing the actual band live and in videos. Vocal-ly, his strength lies in his ability to belt out the powerful stuff. Songs like Best of You, All My Life, *and* Pretender *are in his wheel house. He can shift to the "singing" side of the music, but seemed to be restraining himself at times and looked almost eager to return to belting it out as soon as he could. Banter be-tween songs was fun, but again not the strongest part of his performance.*

"The combo of Chris Beltran on guitar and KC Peters playing bass is worth noting in that not only do both men perform superbly as backing vocal-ists under Johnson, but also play with a ferocity that will have your forearms aching in sympathy by the end of the night. They stay in time and provide a sound that is much richer than what you expect. Seriously, this quartet creates a wall of sound that pastes you to the wall.

"I saved drummer Christian Smith for last with good reason. Portland's Tribute Band scene has some pretty Incredible drummers I could rattle off a list of names and have you nodding in appreciation. Well, add Smith to that list. Watch AND LISTEN to him during Walk...*the way he keeps immaculate time is something to behold. He is a muscle car engine that pounds with ferocity and skill.*

"*By the time that they closed (with the song* Monkey Wrench*), I had been converted from interested to HUGE FAN. As soon as the last chord drifted away, Denise looked at me and said, "Wow, those guys are fun and it really shows that they love doing this." Then she swooned a bit over the skills and the performance of Christian Smith. (What can I say, my wife has a thing for drummers...and the guitarists for Lovedrive.) These guys want to play and it is obvious that they REALLY enjoy themselves doing it. That is perhaps the strongest endorsement that I can give.*"

With Jon Johnson taking guitar and vocals, he has quite a challenge. This is a band that can't really try to adopt a certain look to bring the fans the experience. It will rely heavily on the dynamic vocals that were laid down by Dave Grohl. This is a challenge that he is more than happy to tackle. If you are not overly familiar with the Foo sound, simply play the track *All My Life*. That ought to give you an idea of how much of a vocal challenge it is to pull off the Foo Fighters with any degree of success. I had to come out of the gate and ask Jon Johnson what the hardest song in their catalog was for him to pull off.

Jon Johnson (guitar/lead vocals): "It's usually the ones towards the end of the set when my voice is almost gone (laughs). You know, Foo Fighters is awesome. It's a rock band, and so, I'm not afraid of any of their songs. That's just because we've spent a lot of time practicing and we spend a lot of time trying to be true to the music. I think when you go see the Foo live...I saw them at the Salem Armory for the first time (the *One by One* Tour) in around 2003 and I just remember that entire Salem Armory pit was just rockin' the entire time. It was one of the best raw energy shows that I'd ever seen in my life. That is what we try to re-capture. Of course I've seen them almost every tour since and if you see them now...I know this happens, like, look at David Lee Roth and other lead singers. They are not always able to hit everything. If you listen to a Foo Fighters' album, in the studio, obviously it's incredible. Then you go see 'em live and Dave (Grohl) doesn't sing every word note-for-note. It's impossible to. I've talked to other singers, and if you try to do that, you're gonna lose your voice. Even if you're out there doing it every couple of weeks like we do...in rehearsal, I'll still try to push it as hard as I can. By the end of rehearsal, my back's killing me and my voice is gone. It's because we try to capture it for the fans. Dave Grohl can get away with not singing every note. Monkey Wrench wants to recapture as close as possible that studio experience, and at the same time that awesome raw rock-and-roll live experience that I felt in 2003 at the Salem Armory when I said 'Damn, that's what I want to do!' And so, to capture both of those elements we have to really put in, I think, that extra effort. There's a lot of high screaming, yelling songs that Dave does, and I try to hit that studio quality sound as much as I can."

Chris Beltran (guitars): "There is a lot of time in planning our set list 'cause we're always looking to and thinking about JJ and his voice and what's gonna happen at the end of the night."

The guys from Monkey Wrench are already stepping in to a market that has an act doing the Foo Fighters, but they don't see that as a problem. Their concerns are to simply bring the best experience that they can achieve to the people who come watch them play.

We only briefly touched on that and Chris Beltran shared some advice that they received from Dan Bates (Maiden NW) one night when they went out to take a look at this other band. "It doesn't matter how many Tribute Bands of the same band there are, just make sure you're the best."

Johnson: "Chris Beltran is really focused on being true to the music. We're musicians, we've all been in other bands and are still doing other stuff (original music), and we're fans of the music, so we're not gonna do something we can't do and do it right. I think one of Chris's comments is our tag line: 'We're the Pacific Northwest's Foo Fighter's Tribute Band…hear the difference.' We say that because you're gonna hear a difference, and it's gonna be in the effort that we put into that true sound. All the fills that Christian (Smith) does on the drums make a huge difference because not everybody is gonna do that…they're just sitting back there keeping time but we put as much effort as we can in those little details."

Advice is something that is often unsolicited. However, if seeking to be better at what you do, it is always best to turn to those who are seeing success in your chosen field. As with all the performers I spoke to, I asked relative newcomers, Monkey Wrench, to share what they believed a good Blueprint for Success to be if you are trying to make it as a Tribute Band.

Johnson: "I say first be true to your music as a musician. Practice and play…but you've gotta love who you're playing. We talked about doing a Pearl Jam Tribute Band with some other guys just because we wanted to keep expanding our musical horizons, but5 you've gotta totally love what you are doing. It doesn't matter if you are playing Harefest or if you're playing a dive bar in North Portland with just your parents and a couple of your friends sitting in front of ya, you've gotta have a great time doing it. We've been doing live music for a while and have played some dive bars but we don't give a fuck if there's nobody out there but the bartender and the guy that's giving us five bucks…we're gonna give him the best show that we can because we love playing the music. So I would say the blueprint is love what you're doing and that passion for what you are doing is real. People are gonna sense it…feel it, and you're gonna be successful no matter if there's nobody out there and you're just having a good time."

Beltran: "Yeah, I definitely think it's the first thing that JJ hit on, and it is the same thing that even Jason talks about to anybody that he would ask in. The first thing he always says is to make sure you do it for fun and that it is what you want to do. The second thing I would add to that is the attention to the details. If you're doing this stuff because you want to be a Tribute Band and not just a garage band is, are you really working towards reproducing the song the way it was recorded…all the nuances. Ninety percent of the people that are listening to you are probably not musicians and are not going to catch these nuances…but there is a feeling that, if you're doing it the way that the actual artist does…that what comes along with that is just this inherent emotion and quality of that sound. The average listener might not realize technically what you're doing, but they feel it and they can hear it versus a band that thinks they can get by with just doing a lick that kinda sounds like it because it's easier."

Christian Smith (drums): "For me, that was the big difference in coming from Over the Edge. We called ourselves a "party rock" band and played cover songs from many different artists. We were just there to give people a good time. Going to a Tribute Band was really about attention to detail. I spent a lot of time going through each of the songs, transcribing the drum licks, watching things live…kinda bouncing things back and forth from any of the professional sources that I could use. That was just as a base to try and get down what I should be playing. The next part was kind of watching what was done live to recreate some of the movements, because that just gets you more in the mode. As you start to get in there and you're feeling it…then you're not only playing the song, but you are inside what the musician was trying to bring across. That is just an awesome feeling and it kind of pours out in the performance that you give. The other thing about getting into a Tribute Band is that you're (typically) studying one artist at a time. You not only know the song, but you also learn the tendencies of the artists themselves based off of just the repeated licks and fills and things like that that you see kind of come up again and again. For me, it's trying to be perfect every night, but also making sure that I'm not so focused on perfection that the performance is suffering."

When you don't have or need flashy costumes, the music becomes an even bigger part of the show. That is not to say that the music is not crucial with each Tribute Band, that is simply stating that as some of the acts of the 90's become the target of Tribute Bands, it will not even be a question of looking the part. You just better damn well sound like it.

TRIBUTE

13

"Hey, Ladies!"

James Brown sings, "It's a man's world…" and when you are talking about the rock music landscape, there is a sad lack of curves that point to that statement being overwhelmingly true. Before you throw your hands up in disgust, name ten major female acts of the 80's rock scene…okay, extend it to the 70's. Still don't have ten? Then you see what I am simply pointing out.

I love groups like Vixen, The Runaways, and Femme Fatale, but I also know that some of you may only have even actually heard of one of those groups. You may not know that The Runaways spun off Joan Jett and Lita Ford.

Now, if I mention Heart or Pat Benatar, I bet you are all nodding. They were probably in that list you just started creating a moment ago.

The Tribute Scene is no different, and in some ways, a caricature of the rock music genre as a whole. That also means that this book lacks when it comes to representing the female influence. Lucky for me, I was able to track down Donna Caruk at her home in the Great White North—also known as Canada—where she is preparing to pay the Pacific Northwest a visit as the singer for Barracuda (she also plays a mean flute just in case you haven't caught their show yet), a remarkable Heart Tribute Band. Even more exciting, she will be front and center for a Pat Benatar Tribute Band as well (both to be featured at Harefest 6).

We wasted no time getting down to the top item on my list as she shared her ideas on a Blueprint for Success involving Tribute Bands.

Donna Caruk (Ann Wilson vocals): "I think the most important thing is to be able to do the job and do it right. I've seen a lot of really bad Tributes, and if you want to be successful, you have to do your homework. You have to at least sound (or look) like the person…one or the other. I mean, not everybody has the gift of having both, but you have to have something that connects the public to the music you're doing. Anybody can get up and pretend to be Elvis, Roy Orbison, or Heart, but if there's nothing that the audience can connect with when they come and see you, then it's not going to be accepted."

With fewer choices when it comes to acts that women can perform if they are staying true to the band's gender, there are a number of hurdles and obstacles that female performers face that go beyond just the music. This involves even more creativity, and the willingness to even forgo what many would consider the basics.

Caruk: "I think the biggest hurdle, and we still encounter it, is (the idea) that women don't rock, or Heart doesn't rock. That's a big one. Heart has a lot of really pretty acoustic stuff, and I think a lot of people just don't get it until we actually hit the stage and they see us. There is a misconception for some reason that Heart doesn't rock, and it has been a detriment because people will pass over us for something that they think is heavier. And there aren't a lot of women's Tributes. One of the other problems is that we picked two artists that are still touring in the area (Heart and Pat Benatar) which sometimes doesn't help because the real guys are going to be coming to town. Then there is the personal hurdle…a lot of times there is not a proper changing room with a mirror and good lighting. Being a female artist, you kind of need a little more prep work. A lot of the guys will come kind of dressed, and we don't really have the opportunity to do that. We have to put on our makeup and stuff. Last year, we did it in this park we played using the maintenance room with a riding lawn mower, gas cans, and there was a sink there with a little mirror, so they said, 'Okay, use this.' (laughs) They never have anything really set up for women…so we get to use the public wash room."

It might seem like no big deal, but many of the fans who attend these events really do not understand how much mental preparation goes into taking the stage. To be trying to slip into your outfit as people parade in and out of the wash room is distracting. If you add in the likelihood that there will be people who want to chat, ask questions, and just genuinely gush about how amazing the performers are, it makes that level of focus difficult to attain. Make no mistake, the performers enjoy meeting the fans, but it is much more enjoyable *after* they have performed versus just before they are about to do so.

Not that there will be any openings any time soon in Barracuda, but it is always good to know what sorts of skill and demeanor are most sought after by performers. When asked, I got a very succinct laundry list.

Caruk: "What we have learned over the years is that communication is one of the biggest things. Being able to get along with your peers and not be narcissistic would be the second. That is sometimes more important than skill or talent. If you hate being on stage or being at rehearsal with a person, then it's really not worth it...of course you have to be able to hone your skills and do a good job, but I think that, above all, if a band is going to be successful and longevity is going to come into play, then you have to be able to get along with people...you have to communicate, do your homework, you have to commit. I think a lot of players talk a good game, but they can't follow through."

There is also another aspect to the Tribute Band arena that sees even less attention and is often overlooked. That would be when a woman or group of women take on an artist that is male. Examples would be Hells Belles, an all-female AC/DC tribute.

Then there is Diva Lee Roth.

She stood out front of the Van Halen Tribute, Drop Dead Legs in the Diamond Dave persona. What I found interesting when doing some research was the degree of vitriol that is spewed on social media at a woman fronting this act. I tribute Diva's belief in herself and her ability to not let the general mean-spiritedness that can exist so prevalently online dissuade her from doing what she loves: entertain.

As far as offering up advice to anybody considering the Tribute Band path, she rings the same bell that has become a theme when speaking to the performers in the Portland scene.

Diva Lee Roth (DLR vocals): "I think you just have to commit. You have to find musicians who will all share the same passion and find people who have the same goal as you. I know when I started (with Drop Dead Legs), Van Halen was not my passion, however, I *love* to entertain. So my passion came from loving the stage, loving to sing, loving to dance, and I think David Lee Roth was the perfect male for me to tribute. He's so flamboyant...he's very feminine and dancy and extreme. I thought, *I can do that*. I can get my Spandex collection, I have furry leg warmers, I have the gear and, my God, it was so much fun getting on stage...stepping out of me and into a person who I feel has been so much bigger than me. And it was really fun to emulate this huge personality. I loved it. A passion has got to be there whether it is a passion for guitar, or for learning solos...passion for entertaining...a passion for whatever."

If you ask her what she believes will make a woman successful in this heavily male-dominant field, she is very clear.

Diva: "I think what will make a woman successful is staying true to the band that they are trying to imitate and doing it well. It is harder for women to get out on stage and do a Tribute because the female bands are just so much harder. Also, women are harder on women, so there are more women who will come out and see female shows. They are going to know all the tunes by Heart and Joan Jett and the Go-Go's. That's stuff that, growing up an 80's child, I know that stuff inside and out. So when I go see a band, the women are the bitchiest in the crowd. That was one of my biggest fears coming in as a female doing a tribute to Van Halen…it was very stressful for me. It made me question if I was doing the right thing. But once the music started, all of that was gone. I just went out and did my thing and had so much fun doing it. But…I always did have the question in the back of my mind because I would be criticized far more than a male."

When asked for her take on why there were not more female acts out there and if it was the minute number of female acts, or perhaps just a lack of women willing to put themselves out there in this field, Diva said, "I think it's a mix. But it's going to take the musicianship and the talent. I think maybe there is not the demand."

Donnie Lee Roth (from Unchained): "One thing to consider, is if there are enough hits in their catalog. You can't really build a tribute band around a one-hit-wonder type band. You've got to be able to play 'at least' a solid ninety-minute set of hits and/or really well known songs. That can be 20-25 songs. Take *Jaime's Cryin'* for instance. Everyone knows that song, but it was never a 'hit', never charted, but when we play it everyone knows the lyrics. Van Halen was just one of those bands that, even their B-side songs, were generally popular. If you need an example, take a look at the bands on the J-Fell roster. All of the bands Jason Fellman promotes has this trait in common."

(A combo consisting of The Runaways, Joan Jett, and Lita Ford was lobbed in the air during the conversation.)

Diva: "The variety of that kind of show would be super awesome. I mean, when you come for a Van Halen show, you are a fan…but there are also people that are like, 'Aww, that's all you do?' I tell them I do a lot of different things…at different shows. But when you put yourself in any of those roles, you damn well better sell yourself. I felt like I had an extra battle on my hands (as David Lee Roth's character), and it was a problem for me for a long time. I don't have his voice, I can fake it, I can work on sounding like him, I can work on having his inflections and using his innuendoes and I can make it happen. However, I'm not a dude, so you can't really compare me to the real thing other than the energy and the show."

Whether they are taking on female rock icons such as Heart, Pat Benatar, and Joan Jett, or stepping into a male role, there can be no doubt that the women have a more difficult path to tread. Fortunately, there are a few ladies out there willing to undertake that journey.

14

For Those About to Rock

You never know who you might bump into at a Tribute Band concert. You might just bump into a *USA Today* or even *Forbes* sports columnist. If you catch the AC/DC Tribute Band that goes by the name Shoot to Thrill, you will see that very same columnist step into the Malcolm Young role as the rhythm guitarist and backing vocalist. He and drummer Kevin Rankin were both kind enough to share some time with me as they prepared for an upcoming Harefest kickoff party as well as the big event that would come just a month later.

Before I share some of the thoughts they offered on the Tribute Band scene here in Portland, as well as some helpful pointers to those of you who might be considering that path, I wanted to share a portion of one of my reviews regarding my experience at a Shoot to Thrill concert.

"*So, normally I give the lowdown on the show I saw by talking about the opener and then the headliner. Not this time. When I saw the band Shoot to Thrill for the first time, it was at the Canby Harefest. I will openly admit that I had two very distinct reactions. Musically, I thought that they were the tightest band to perform when it came to the music. However, I was not as enthusiastic about the lead singer. Evan Berry is a talented young man, of that I had no doubt, but I have seen the original lineups (meaning both Bon Scott and Brian Johnson) in the flesh. Evan's vocals were too modern. He was a bit of a screamer, whereas, Bon was nasty sex and Brian was a punch in the face.*

"*A few months later, I entered the Aladdin with no new expectations. I will say on the record that Evan has grown into his role, and if he continues to show this sort of amazing growth, then he will own any true AC/DC fan's admiration. He came out and took control of the stage and belted out vocals in a way that made me wonder what spirit he was channeling. He had an edgy nastiness when he took on AC/DC classics from the Bon Scott era and then snarled out the Brian Johnson lyrics with a voice twice the size of the young man I had seen just a few short months ago.*

"The rest of the band is still just as tight as I remember. Ted Berry IS Angus Young (as well as Evan's dad) and he is a ball of energy that will make you wonder what fountain of youth he drinks from before the show. Maury Brown holds down the rhythm as Malcolm Young (with one of the most beautiful guitars I have seen in a while) and Jeff Krebs drives the rhythm engine on bass along with Kevin Rankin on the drums as Cliff Williams and Phil Rudd respectively. If you are in the Northwest and have never seen the power and glory of an AC/DC concert, or, if you just want to re-live the glory of one of rock's premiere bands, then go to the J-Fell page and find out when and where you can see them next. Fair warning, this show sold out...and I see that as a trend that will continue for a long time. And let me just say to Evan Berry...young man, you have converted me into a fan."

Shoot to Thrill has perhaps one of the local Tribute Band scene's youngest members in their front man, Evan Berry. His potential for growth is wide open, and each time that I have seen these guys, he has only gotten better at slipping into his split-personality of Bon Scott and Brian Johnson.

If you are one of the people reading this to find perhaps a nugget or two of good information about how to successfully build your own Tribute Band, here are two guys that have played to sold out houses all over town, and in some cases...around the world. I think they know a thing or two about doing it right.

Maury Brown (guitar): "We have a huge advantage in that we tribute a band that has been vastly popular for many decades. You can tribute any band because you enjoy it, first and foremost. But the biggest thing, if you want to be able to be popular...I like to think we do it well, but if you pick a band like AC/DC or Led Zeppelin or Journey, those bands have humongous followings. That really helps. Try and perform it as close as you can to the original...have the nuance in it. If there is a performance element and an entertainment element to it, you want to look like that band as much as possible. Try to be true to the band that you're tributing as much as possible. Pick a band that has significant popularity with a large, broad catalog."

Kevin Rankin (drums): "Don't go into it just expecting to make money. It's gonna show on stage. So, go into the project with some sort of appreciation and fascination with the artist you're going to pay tribute to. Spend a lot of time studying the persona for each character in that band. If you're trying to emulate...say...the Scorpions...and you don't have a singer (like Larry Smith of Lovedrive) who can pull off a great Klaus, don't even try. There's no way that you're going to convince someone that this is the Scorpions if they close their eyes. If they're genre specific, maybe take a look at their wardrobe. Maybe study all the transitions and evolutions of that band's persona. So if they started off real glam and Spandex-y in the 80's and they evolved into denim and leather in the 90's (like Bon Jovi), then study what their wardrobe and hairstyles looked like. You really have to think about what the audience experience is and give every attention to detail to that paying audience. Make sure the entire ensemble of guys that you have can fit the persona, and make sure there is an investment already in place for that signature guitar or that double bass drum set if that band had it. Hairstyles...you're gonna have to do the wigs, and you may have to invest a couple hundred bucks in a decent real-hair wig. Then you have a stylist match you up as close as possible to that band so you don't go out there looking like you're playing at some Halloween joke show."

Brown: "Spend the extra time on that one artist to really try and get every little nuance. The bands that spend the extra time to really get it down and close to the original...those bands really rise to become the cream of the crop."

If you talk to the people playing around Portland, you do hear a common theme being shared when it comes to how well the bands get along. That may be another reason that they are all so successful. If you are in a market where it is cut-throat and dirty, perhaps try to foster that sense of brotherhood. After all, it's not like you are going to be out there playing every night. The fans will benefit if there are not only a vast number of choices, but a selection of *good* choices.

Rankin: "The really cool thing about this local scene, and I think in what Jason has done, he's found the niches that needed to be filled and sort of arranged a package of genre specific and band specific bands that will fit a bill. You might have Bon Jovi, Journey, and Foreigner Tributes all on the same bill. That's really appealing to the same market."

Much like the band that they pay tribute to, Shoot to Thrill is about the longevity of the scene. They are a top-notch act that fills large venues and enjoy the rewards of their hard work by playing in front of crowds that more often than not number in the thousands, not the tens. With a singer growing into his role, the future is bright.

TRIBUTE

15

Counterpoint

In high school, one of my dreams was to be a journalist. My instructor told me time and again that I had a real knack for digging into things and finding a story worth telling. I never did follow that dream, but I did jump headfirst into the whole author thing. I say this because I want to make it clear that I am NOT a journalist. I chose this project as my "non-zombie" offering on the year. It is being done because I really do love the Tribute Band scene and want to share it with you.

Until the interviews started, I really had no clue what my "angle" was going to be. As I spoke with more and more of the performers, I found that maybe I could cobble together some words of advice from people who have been successful at making a name for themselves in the local Tribute Band circuit.

As the book took shape, I realized there was something missing. I needed a counterpoint. Not that I want or desire to punch holes in Tribute Bands. I simply want to offer up the thoughts of a performer NOT playing in a Tribute Band.

One of my little discoveries during the information gathering phase was that most of the Tribute Band performers either have been or are currently doing original music projects as well. They openly admit that, if they perform live with their original project bands, the attendance is a very small fraction of the numbers that they see doing their Tribute Band shows.

Not that I need a disclaimer, but, I feel it is important to offer this side without a filter. Whether I agree or disagree with the statements that I have collected from the array of performers that I was fortunate enough to interview, I shared *their* words. That same courtesy is given to a performer who is not part of the Tribute Band picture.

I spoke with local performer, Thomas Andersen to get a bit of input from somebody who is solely trying to carve his way through the local music landscape playing nothing but original music. As with most of the Tribute perform-ers, Andersen is in more than one band (Lightning Kings, $INTAX) and stays rather busy doing what he loves. We jumped straight in as he shared his take on the Tribute Bands.

Thomas Andersen (guitar): "There's three parts of this whole Tribute thing, and I've kinda come full circle. Not just in my attitude about it, but the understanding. I think acceptance was the hardest thing at first. One part of this is the bands, the second is the fans, and third is the overall effect on the mu-sic...I want to say 'business' but I will use that term lightly. I say that because the business model is broken in the way it used to be and in the way it effects original artists. I have a unique viewpoint because I also played in a Tribute at one time, years ago before they were popular, or at least at the level of populari-ty that they are now which is just astounding."

Now that he had his talking points, I sat back and let him sort through those three points he mentioned. He started with the bands.

Andersen: "Ninety-nine percent of the bands that do these Tributes are of the top-notch, highest caliber of professionals that I've ever known. That was a curiosity to me at first. I got the whole part of it where they eked out a living, they found a niche to collect a paycheck. They're having fun and you can't shake a stick at that. Some of them were in bands that were completely over-looked, and now they've got a moment in the sun and are putting a hundred and ten percent into it. And let's face it...it's entertaining. It is some of the most entertaining nights that I've had in years. To go out and see Iron Maiden (the Tribute version) for ten bucks? Then there's the one percent...guys that should just not be doing it (Tributes). But we're not gonna talk about them. I'm more interested in the ones that are at least fairly accurate, or in some cases better."

He spoke briefly about guitar players specifically. His views are that other guitar players that come to these shows would/will be the most difficult people to please and impress.

Andersen: "Guitar players, as a breed, are the hardest patrons to please. They're the guys out in the audience with their arms crossed. You better have your stuff together. If you're trying to pull off Randy Rhodes chops and they're half-assed...you're done in their eyes. But you look at the Journey Tribute (Stone in Love), that guy (Davin) is a phenom. He's an incredible guitar player. To cover that stuff at the intensity that they do, and stay as true to it as they do is remarkable. I don't know how the fuck they do it. It's too much for me to even comprehend. I mean, how do you spend that much time figuring out someone else's style...every little mannerism, every little nuance in the mu-sic...it's just mind-boggling. That one percent that shouldn't be doing it, not to spend much time talking about it, but there were just a few things that stuck in my craw. The ones that sell merch, but this goes to the image and likeness thing, and the intellectual property of music. That's the part I don't understand...how that's okay. That is what actually started the decline in the music business in the first place, which led to this Tribute movement, which is ironic. Think back to when those lines of intellectual property were blurred by Napster, there was a scramble. Metallica led the way and they turned out to be hated for it by a general misunderstanding public. Everything that was said by them back then about Napster and the music business actually happened. There are no more metal deals, there are no more being signed to a record label. That whole business model is gone forever. It makes you wonder about the direction of music. What's gonna happen in three decades? Who is gonna be tribute then? Everything is tour-based now."

Andersen: "The second part is the fans. The fans are really the key and the answer. They (the Tribute Bands) are a comfortable slipper for the middle-aged crowd, that demographic forty to sixty. There's no surprises, no raised expectations for the general concert goer. The price is right and they get to see stuff they grew up (listening) to. That's really the key to the success of the whole thing. There's still an audience alive that wants to hear it. But twenty years from now, it won't be pretty. But at this point in time, it's national. Hell, there's a television show about it."

We then just sort of spoke briefly about my vision for this book. Also, after he apologized for "going off on a diatribe" during our interview, I reassured him that I felt it was important for "the other side" to be on display. Every side has two stories. Talk to an original musician who is not part of the Tribute Band scene and the responses can be anywhere from accepting to openly hostile. Andersen's views were never expressed with any sort of anger, simply a certain degree of what sounded like apprehension.

Andersen: "My primary counterpoint is: "What about the future?" We don't really think about that when we are at a Tribute show. We're there to reunite with old friends, listen to old music that we're familiar with. It's not intrusive. It's not gonna shock us. That is what the whole movement was based on, and that's why it's thriving. Aside from the fact that this market happens to have the talent and the well-versed marketing strategist in the form of J-Fell (Jason Fellman). I have to give him credit, that guy is smart...there's no two ways about it. He figured it out, he brought the bands together, he saw the niche in the market and he created a business. He brings entertainment to a lot of people. At that level, those bands are super lucky that they have him, because there aren't a lot of promoters in the first place. Some national tour bands don't have that kind of representation."

There can be no denying that, by and large, the Tribute Band shows draw larger crowds. The question had to be asked. Can the Original Band music scene survive or have the Tributes put it on the endangered species list? How is it faring here locally?

Andersen: "There are some fantastic local, original bands…it's actually bigger now than it was twenty years ago. It's gone back underground because there's no huge audience for it. The audience is now out there for Tribute Bands…if you come to a local band show, you're gonna see forty people. You go to a local Tribute Band show, you're gonna see four hundred and forty people. It's just a fact. Early on, it got personal. But they (Original Bands) just need to be thinking about how to organize…to manipulate this space and time in your life in order to better and move forward with your art rather than pointing at someone else and saying that they're the reason for your problems. The tribute scene has been accused by many crying original artists to have 'poisoned' the water, forcing them to give up on music all together…I say it has actually purified the water because now the ranks are thinned out and only the true original artist remain…all is now as it should be. My bands have actually benefited in some ways because the tribute bands liked us and supported us by putting us on the bill with them. Of course the audience was not there for us, but we won them over one t-shirt and cd at a time."

This book is about shining some light on a genre of live music that I have a bit of a love affair with. I felt it was also important to talk to a local artist not currently involved in a Tribute Band just to get a little more perspective. I have urged you regularly to check out these acts for yourself (in your area, wherever that may be). I also want to take this opportunity to say the same when it comes to the local Original Bands playing around town.

16

Wanted: Dead or Alive

In the 80's, I was one of those guys who openly mocked Bon Jovi. After all, he was just too damn pretty. He had THE perfect hair coupled with a thousand mega-watt smile that made girls go crazy. My outward beef was that he was "Living on his Hair". (That was my Weird Al twist on the Bon Jovi hit *Living on a Prayer*. I know, not very creative, but I was only sixteen or seventeen for crying out loud…give me a break!)

That was my outward reaction.

When I was all alone where none of my high school gang of Priest/Maiden/Ozzy/Scorps-loving headbangers could catch me, I was belting out *Dead or Alive* and *Blaze of Glory* at the top of my lungs. My appreciation of that band stayed hidden with the same feelings I had for Thompson Twins, Duran Duran, and INXS. Fast forward to today where I can listen to whatever I want and not care. At last, I could express my true feelings for the boys from Jersey.

The first time that I saw local Tribute Band Steelhorse, I was hooked. The second time was even better and this is an excerpt of the review from that show—a double-bill with Steelhorse and Shoot to Thrill:

"Steelhorse is the band I came to the Aladdin theater to see. This is another band that I saw for the first time at the Canby Harefest this past August. When I was younger and Bon Jovi was popular, I actually dismissed them because I was into Motley Crüe, Van Halen, and KISS. I saw Bon Jovi as too pretty to like. However, the Young Guns *song,* Blaze of Glory, *converted me. Then I found out that this was the same band that had put out the track* Runaway *a few years earlier. So I wiped the egg off my face and gave them another listen. After that, they were sort of my dirty secret.*

"Mark Thomas fronts this band and if you are not right next to him, you

would swear that Jon Bon Jovi snuck onstage. He is simply amazing and has some crazy good vocals. However, this is the band that was a too-close-to-call second when it came to the tightness of their sound onstage. That has to be credited to Bryan Harvey on keyboards, Jeff Buehner on bass and Kevin Rankin on drums providing a soundtrack. Yep, Kevin Rankin pulled double duty that night. After a flawless set behind Steelhorse, he drove the bus for Shoot to Thrill. J-Fell knows how to put together one helluva night for music fans. I will say that Jeff is one of the most enthusiastic and expressive bass players on the tribute scene (and alongside Motorbreath's Mark Trees, could probably become the next WWE tag team champions of the world).

"I saved a special part to talk about a very talented guitarist. The first time that I saw Brian McGroovy (how cool is that name?!) was with a Cult tribute band. He just exudes "cool". He is one of those guys that you watch play that makes you believe that playing the guitar is easy. Make no mistake...it is NOT. However, he is just that damn good. He is charismatic and plays with style. I think I have a slight man-crush on this guy. Not in the scary, stalker way, just in the "hanging out with this guy would be freakin' awesome" sort of way."

Several of the members of Steelhorse gave me some of their time and we talked about what it takes to put a band like this together and pull it off so successfully. Then...well, then we just talked about whatever came up. Surprisingly, the biggest statements came about the business end of this scene. If you are trying to get a foot in the door, this is probably where you want to pay serious attention.

Kevin Rankin (drums): "You had mentioned that some of your chapters may sort of come off as 'love letters' to certain bands, but there are certain bands in town that deserve that dedication. I know you've interviewed a lot of the bands in the scene, and it would be pretty easy to feel like we're unique in this community. There are a lot of cities that have a good Tribute thing happening, but the difference, and I bet you've heard it over and over again, is that Jason Fellman and the J-Fell thing really made this a much bigger, thriving community in that demographic. At that same time, you've got other bands coming out of the woodwork, trying to put together a Tribute that don't get his model. And maybe they are trying to pay a tribute to a band they love, but they don't understand business...the niche that they're filling. So maybe they're pissed that they're stuck playing a Wednesday night at a back street pub and they can't get into the Aladdin Theater or the Roseland. I've heard it over and over how so many guys dog the J-Fell network as being this monopoly in this scene. Those guys don't get it...they don't understand the business and they feel like they can't get those gigs because Jason has a hold of them. The fact of the matter is that Jason offers a really competitive product. He offers venues an opportunity to make money. The venues aren't gonna bring bands in because

Jason's a nice guy, they're packing bands in because they know they're gonna make money off of it...fill the seats and sell drinks. A lot of these bands don't understand that, if they can't command a draw of three...four...five hundred people, then the venue doesn't want 'em. It doesn't matter who brings the package to them."

That segued into the Bon Jovi choice and the beginning of Steelhorse.

Mark Thomas (vocals): "The Bon Jovi thing...I didn't know if I was going to be able to do that. It is a completely different animal than Guns N' Roses vocally. I thought, well, it'll be fun. I Like the music. We'll see if my voice will even do that. It's kind of like, you jog all the time outside...let's see if swimming is good for my exercise routine. It's good *for* you, let's see if it's something that I can do well. It's worked out alright, but it definitely takes some different disciplines, because it requires more vocal finesse. Where Guns N' Roses is a lot more power and emotion...just balls out."

Rankin: "When Jason came to me, he brought the Bon Jovi idea because it was a niche that hadn't yet been filled. When he (Fellman) put the Stone in Love thing together, he knew from having been in cover bands for so long, that, with a little bit more attention to detail and focusing on making a real authentic tribute to Journey, he knew that he could get this demographic of middle-aged soccer moms that had some expendable money and extra time on their hands, and that they wanted to re-live the days of their youth. Within the span of a year, he put together the show at the Aladdin. I remember going down to the big NAMM (National Association of Music Merchants) show in LA and their (Stone in Love) show being showcased on YouTube and it was the first time that most of the community got a sense of what Stone in Love was all about. The videos made it look much larger than life and everybody in town woke up. So he saw the gap for Bon Jovi, and along with the soccer moms, there were all the guys who secretly loved Bon Jovi, or would gladly go see a Bon Jovi Tribute because they knew that there were women there. I know that sounds a little bit crass, but it's true. I know I'm speaking a little dramatically about this, but it really is like a little escape for them for a few hours where they can go back to that moment and get as close to that Bon Jovi concert that they saw when they were seventeen for a fraction of the price and hopefully get the same kind of feeling. With the look and the sound and the energy all there, that is where a lot of the bands really fail. They don't get that you're selling that package. There's the aesthetic piece, the authenticity, the sound, the energy, and even the banter. That is one thing that Mark from both Appetite (for Deception) and Steelhorse does so well. He studies those old concerts. He looks at what Axl did...what Jon Bon Jovi did...and he'll give at least a tip of the hat to some of the stuff that Jon would say to the audience. He wants people to walk away feeling that, for ten bucks, they got to spend a night watching Bon Jovi, and that we (Steelhorse) were so close to the real thing that it was like that person was eighteen again."

Brian McGroovy (guitar): "A position became available in Steelhorse. And it's not like they put a Craigslist ad out. It was just one of the guys who said, 'Let's get Brian and see if he wants to do it. And then I find myself doing that. I knew two of the guys already and my wife had known the drummer (Rankin) for twenty some years, and I'd known the bass player (Jeff Buehner) for around twenty-five years. So I had references...friend references."

It seems that Steelhorse is a band put together from some of the top talent of other bands also seeing a great deal of success on the Tribute Band stage. This is a perfect group of men to ask about putting together that mystical blue-print when it comes to seeing success.

McGroovy: "I don't know if I have the right answer for it. It's sort of one of those things where you sort of happen upon it. I've been in original bands all my life. This is only in the last four years that I have played in a Tribute Band. I'd never been in cover bands before that...ever. All my bands were originals and one even had a record deal with Universal. It's just, when that band sort of unceremoniously stopped playing, there wasn't anything to do and like with any passion, you don't really want to quit. So, you just kind of happen upon it and get some of your other musician friends that are veterans and say, 'Hey, maybe we should try this and see how it goes.' I don't think there is really a blueprint for it unless you just get a group of guys that...one, are really good players; two, are really driven to make it work and happen. The rest is sorta just rehearsal and making yourself sound exactly right. I liken this to an acting job. I have to get into the character. I've seen some Tributes...I've seen some bands...that may not be playing very much. And I don't mean to sound superfi-cial about it at all, but they don't really seem to put much into the presentation. Like, I gotta go out and wear a hat. If I am going to play Ritchie Sambora, then I better try to look like him as best I can. And that's *secondary* to trying to play like him. When I was asked to play in Steelhorse, I was like, 'Really?' (laughs) 'People want to see that?' And to my surprise, not being a big Jon Bon Jovi fan, there's a whole crowd of people that just love it. I'll play a show and look out there...seeing people that sing along and know every word to every single song, and it's probably because it's their prom song, first date song, their wed-ding,...it's their nostalgia. It's bringing them back to their youth. It's the same for me...probably with other bands." *(Author's note: Brian confessed his fan-dom of the group Devo...which I felt only increased his cool factor by exponential amounts.)*

Rankin: "I'll say that this community would not have what it has now without Jason (Fellman). I get asked all the time, 'How do you guys get these shows?' or 'What's up with Jason?' Because they don't get it. They say, 'How do we start a Tribute Band and not be in the clutches of J-Fell?' They obviously don't know. If you don't want to be in the *clutches* of J-Fell, that means you're probably going to be playing in the lower end gigs. *(Author's note: Specific venues were mentioned, but I chose to leave them out.)* I tell them that if those sorts of places are what you're looking for, then that's fine. I paid those dues long ago and I'm not interested in going back now. Jason has changed this whole music scene…and it's not just the Tribute Band thing. Really, he's focused on developing original acts and seeing where things can improve. He's been involved in music marketing. He does workshops and seminars, but he's also getting involved in Fair Trade music. Trying to get musician parking spaces dedicated at venues. When there's an opportunity to make something better, whether it be experience for venues, or experience for bands, or making a sort of 'boiler plate' marketing plan that Tributes can use to be successful…he's done it. He's paid a lot of money out of his pocket and he's learned a lot of lessons…and lost a lot of money making this thing happen, but he's gained so much from it too. He's not looking for the attention to be all about J-Fell. I would bet that every talent booker at the good venues jumps at the chance to work with him because they know they are getting a professional package. He's not gonna BS them. There's not gonna be any wheelin' and dealin' after the show is over to try and negotiate something different."

Since everybody sees the world through his or her own filter, I was curious to hear what this group believed to be the reason behind such a symbiotic relationship between such a wide variety of performers and personalities.

McGroovy: "I've lived in Portland since around '87, and in that time, being in just original bands, I've been around a lot of other musicians that have become friends. It's been this community of friends really, that has built up over the years. What it feels like to me is this growing community of friends and musicians that have all just decided to do this, and it's sorta been wrapped up in package by Jason Fellman in terms of how he's built this up. I mean, I gave up on the whole idea of becoming a rock star years ago…in the early 90's. It was like, 'Yeah, that's not happening.' So this group of friends and musicians have all sort of congregated into these bands. We still enjoy playing music, you make some money, make people happy while still doing some original stuff if you like."

Drummers are seldom heard from, but Steelhorse has one of the less shy and reserved sort in Kevin Rankin. To close out this segment, I leave you with his take on the difference between a Tribute Band and a cover band for those who might not see one.

Rankin (drums): "People that are outside this scene that have played in cover bands or gone to see cover bands, they might come away from a show saying, "Oh yeah, I saw a Bon Jovi cover band this weekend. I'm always wanting to correct that...a cover band is a totally different thing. Bands that are in that situation (cover band) might play at a bar. They play every Friday and Saturday night and say they play *mostly* Bon Jovi songs. Chances are, the biggest difference is the audience experience that they give at the front end. But the dollar signs, the number of zeroes on the check in the back end are vastly different because people can go out and pay (little or) no cover charge and listen to songs they know by a bar band...but they don't get the experience. That is what we're trying to give...to make sure that it's as close to authentic as possible in look and feel and sound. Then you can command a higher dollar because you've put the work, time, and energy...we've invested a lot in the financial side on our end. Maybe everything you get from the band goes back in to make sure that you have the right gear, the right look, the right outfits."

17

Guitar Heroes, Outtakes, and Hero Worship

Not everything that I gathered during these interviews fit in nice, neat packages. Some of the stuff was simply fun or informative. All of these artists had stories to tell about life on and off the stage. They also have a healthy appreciation for each other. (I will go deeper down that rabbit hole later.) Here are a few musings that I felt worth sharing.

Brian McGroovy (Steelhorse): (On front man Mark Thomas) "He does a good job with it. Mark most of all gets *really* into the character of it. He'll watch videos. You've seen him in Appetite for Deception and he does an amazing job of being Axl in his prime. He'll do the same moves as whoever he's portraying. He does that with Bon Jovi too, and I turn around and look at him and think, 'Man, I'd be really tired if I was jumping around like that.' Perhaps I should do a better job. I think Ritchie Sambora definitely hammed it up a lot more than I am. But he's who he is…lots of experience. For me, at the beginning it was a lot of, 'Okay, I don't play guitar solos.' My original bands didn't require a guitar solo. It was really more about the song as a whole. I pretty much gave up the whole thing about seeing how much faster I could play…the whole Guitar Hero thing. So this was like a big challenge to see if I could still do it. My wife is the one that pushed me into it. (laughs) She said, 'You can do this. People think that you're just a rhythm guitar player.' And I kinda am. So it's like you've been sitting on the couch for twenty years, and next week you're gonna run a marathon."

The following is perhaps a bit vulgar and crass. You can feel free to skip ahead, but I share it simply because it was one of those spontaneous moments that showed the cohesion between the members of Appetite for Deception and how they play off and feed off of each other's energy with such ease. This scene played out after over an hour of sit-down interview time. As guitarist Michael "Izzbo" Killian was excusing himself for the night and heading out, I pointed out the guitar that I am collecting signatures on from members of the Tribute Bands.

Michael "Izzbo" Killian (Appetite for Deception): "Where do you want it?" (holding the guitar and the Sharpie)

Me: (Obviously not thinking) "Anywhere you put it."

Izzbo: "Hey, I love to hear that!" (falsetto voice) "Wherever you wanna put it…not in there!"

Andrew "Sorum" Greene: "Where would you say the butthole of the guitar is?"

Mark Thomas: "The guitar's back!"

Izzbo: "I would say it's its knee!"

This was just one instance of how simple banter led off on a tangent. It shows the Appetite for Deception crew as being just what they claim to be. Just a bunch of guys who are lucky enough to be doing something that they love. What is not included is that immediately after this moment of levity, they reverted to all business as they mapped out upcoming rehearsal times before a few of the members departed for the night.

The talent pool can't be denied in the Tribute Band scene. Many of these artists play in original projects as well as their Tribute Bands. One guitarist provided his own thoughts as to the rewards of playing in a Tribute in comparison to his own original projects.

Steve Adams (Ramble On): "Another aspect about Tribute Bands is, having performed my own music…you never get immediate response…emotional, impactive, immediate response from the audience like you do in the Tribute Band. That music…sometimes the audience is going crazy. And you don't get that when you're playing your own music (laughs). It's that symbiosis of performing for that audience…that experience is the primary mover. I guarantee you, most of the guys, when you get down to it…that's a powerful feeling. You don't want to let that go."

If you are just one of the fans of the Tribute Bands and not a person looking for some helpful advice on how to make it into the Tribute Band scene, then it may interest you to know that these guys are music fans just like you. Appetite for Deception shared a story about when one of their own got to meet his icon during an event where they were opening for the actual 80's band, Cinderella. Yet another layer of this group of talented musicians is revealed.

Thomas: "So we get our big cooler full of drinks and this great big sandwich platter and all this stuff."

Greene: "Then the booker said, 'Is there anything else I can get you?' and I jokingly said, 'Can we meet Cinderella?' He says he was supposed to meet 'em in a minute anyway for something."

Thomas: "We were already backstage, so it was basically just getting out of our vehicle and walking over there. So we stood at the side of their bus and were talking to them about the tour…asking Jeff LaBar what they do on the bus and he says, 'You know…we've been watching the Olympics a lot.' Andrew, one of his drumming idols growing up was Fred Coury (Cinderella drummer) and so we get done with our conversation and head back to get something to drink, make a sandwich or whatever and I see Andrew sitting on the couch and he was just looking straight ahead eating his sandwich. He had this reflective look…like a little kid…like an eight-year old sitting there eating and I can see the gloss on his eyes starting to show up. and I'm like, 'Are you crying?' And he was like, 'Shut up! Shut up, dude!' And I thought that was the coolest thing that I've ever seen. I called it a 'Beatles moment' where you're having that frantic fan, euphoric…I don't know what else to call it, because he was having that thing where he'd met his idol and spoke to him and connected…walked away and then had to realize what it meant."

Greene: "It hit me pretty hard."

Thomas: "I mean, I don't know what it meant to him, but I could *see* what it meant to him."

And that seems like a good place to say goodbye to our friends…the men and women who work so hard to entertain us. What follows next are a little bit of my own "fanboy" observations as well as some interesting stuff that I gathered in an off-the-record question.

So, let's jump into the off-the-record question first. I will preface it by saying that this part of the book almost did not happen. The reason was simple…if you ask a large group of people a poll-like question and the answer is unanimous…there isn't much to talk about. Or is there?

The question was a simple one that I thought would be just a fun way to get the bands to talk about the other acts that are in the scene. It went something like this: If you could bump one guy from his slot in the Portland Tribute Band scene, who would it be? What band is it that you watch and think, *Wow, I would love to be a part of that act!*

The question is pretty simple. What I did not expect was to have Appetite for Deception become almost the unanimous answer. In particular, Brandon Cook was singled out as a guitarist and Mark Thomas as a front man.

That tells me that Appetite for Deception is obviously doing something right. They have the respect of their fellow performers in the local area. Other acts see them as a benchmark and a band that is doing it right.

Having spent some quality time with the band, I can say that I see why. They do have an exceptional vibe and there is a very high level of attention to details that make them stand out. That is in no way a slight to any of the other bands that I spent time with and even those that I did not; it is simply stating that Appetite for Deception is doing something at a high level and it is noticed by their friends and comrades in the Tribute Band arena. Fortunately, as I was able to speak with a wider number of performers in the Portland Tribute Band population, non-Appetite for Deception members finally made the list.

Eventually, some other names and acts were mentioned. It really should come as no surprise that Steelhorse made the list. Once again, Mark Thomas has created a role and the band has formed a tight cohesion that makes their show something special.

Rich Ray was singled out simply because so many people say that his voice is "golden" and one of the best vocally in the scene. Whether he is portraying Robert Plant of Led Zeppelin or Lou Gramm of Foreigner, his vocal talent will give you chills.

Bass player Rickey Lepinski is seen as being a ferocious bass player and Kevin Rankin matched Joe Spencer in the realm of drummers. It was nice to see Brad Halleck gain a few nods. His departure was initially pretty tough for me to hear. However, once I met Jim "Top Jimmy" Smoltz, I felt a lot better.

Aside from the players, you might notice that a lot of people in this scene had great things to say about Jason Fellman of J-Fell Presents. It simply can't be denied that he has molded and shaped the local music scene here in Portland. His efforts and hard work do not go unnoticed by the men and women who perform locally. Even bands that are not under his roster acknowledge that he has grown this scene into something that they are able to appreciate and reap the rewards from.

As a person who has stood in the crowd for the past few years, I will say that the level of entertainment received versus the dollar amount spent is a very consumer-friendly ratio. The shows have been a thrill to attend, and I intend to continue doing so for years to come.

18

Look What the Cat Dragged In

Poison'us was the last act the night I saw my very first Tribute Band concert. This was another case of how blown away I was by the degree that a singer could imitate an artist that I was familiar with to such a high degree.

Since that first show, I believe that the wife and I have seen that band more than any of the others except Unchained. Like Unchained and Motorbreath, we have been able to get to know the members away from their stage lives and came to regard them as friends.

This band is a story that really illustrates the cycle of what it takes to build a quality Tribute Band. Since that first show, half of the lineup has changed (the C.C DeVille and Bobby Dall roles). Their reasons are their own and not relevant to this book. What is relevant is that I believe, as an audience member and regular attendee of these shows, that the current band now has the ingredients to take that next step.

Say what you like about Poison, the actual band, but somebody was buying all those albums. Oddly enough, I had no problem openly being a fan of the original band (unlike my secret Bon Jovi thing). Still, this was a band that drew the girls back in the day. Also, they had a certain energy on stage that screamed 'PARTY!'

What follows are a couple of my reviews in regards to their performances. The first one happened in one of those places-that-shall-not-be-named locales. That night was a disaster on the sound end. The team in charge of the PA and soundboard were beyond negligent.

"As many of you know, I am a big fan of the Portland Tribute Band scene. (So much so that I am writing a book about it.) I have caught shows at a number of venues. My love affair began a couple of years ago at a show at [venue omitted]. Sadly, unless the band members are friends, this last Saturday night

might have been the last time I will venture into that establishment. The bands were great...but you would not know that if you relied on the sound board operators (they should ALL be fired!).

"The closing act was Poison'us. We love these guys and have seen them several times. The entire band has been made better by the addition of Roger Jamie on bass as his energy is visibly contagious. (More on him in a bit.) Sadly, the problem was not fixed. Eventually, front man Will "Brett Michaels" Barnes had reached critical mass. He stopped the set; by this point, the hum was creating a tingle in my feet and now you could not hear the guitar of Eric Vanderwall (as C.C. DeVille). The feedback was actually getting worse. Add in the fact that the band could not hear themselves on their monitors, and it was beyond a problem at this point.

"For those not in the know, bands need the monitors, which are speakers aimed their direction, to hear themselves in real time. Otherwise, they would be waiting for the sound to bounce off of the back wall and timing would vanish. No, that loud volume YOU hear is not the same source they use when they play. But, on with this review...

"I got a message from Will Barnes the next day actually apologizing for his "outburst". I wish my "outbursts" were as calm as his was that night. Personally, I think it was tame as well as LONG overdue. Will and the band did like those before them and soldiered on as the crowd just continued to trickle out due to the ineptness of the sound crew at the {location omitted}. They had to improvise when Will's acoustic guitar was not patched in during Every Rose Has Its Thorn, *and yes, the hum remained.*

"Bass player Roger Jamie took on the role of anchor during this show. He gave the band something solid to hang on to as he kept his flamboyant energy at maximum throughout the entire performance. His jokes, witty remarks, and banter with not only the audience, but his fellow band mates kept things from hitting the rocks. Every band should have a Roger Jamie. During his time with Poison'us, we have seen the band transform and become more incredible as his energy is contagious. This guy has a full plate as Gene Simmons in Dr. Love, the KISS tribute band here in Portland, as well as being a professional wrestler."

This was the first time that we saw the band with this new lineup that included Roger Jamie. A short time later, Mick Hassan would join. I was invited to attend that debut. The following Monday, I was able to share my observations in the form of a concert review:

"It is no secret that the long drive was to show support for one of our favorite bands: Poison'us. Recently, I wrote about how adding Roger Jamie on bass had upped the energy and really improved the onstage dynamic of the entire band. And now...they have done it again. Mick Hasson (band mate of Roger

Jamie in Dr. Love—The Northwest's Premiere KISS tribute band) has taken the axe as the new C.C DeVille. One word: WOW!

"So, if you are keeping score, the new lineup is: Will Barnes as Bret Michaels, Mick Hasson as C.C. Deville, Roger Jamie as Bobby Dall, and Andrew Losli as Rikki Rockett. Let's hope they keep it this way. I think they have found the complete package (no pun intended, Mick) with this new lineup. What you now get is the party-fueled experience of the classic Poison concerts. The interaction between all four members of the band is like a party that you somehow got lucky enough to be invited to. All the cool kids are in attendance and they are partying with YOU.

"Will is still spot on in sounding like Brett, and now he has given Roger Jamie a familiar playmate to primp and pose with in true 80's fashion which keeps the audience constantly guessing what might happen next. Even better...now they really sound like classic Poison. It is clear that Mick Hasson makes an effort to reproduce the DeVille sound in a note-for-note manner. That really shows during his solos. He seems to love his role, and it loves him right back.

"Just like the actual band, Poison, this gang has had its detractors, but I think they might give these guys another look. This is now the full package (again, no pun intended, Mick). Andrew Losli is all flare behind the drums as always, and now you actually might miss some of it because of all the onstage antics, but a flurry of activity from behind the kit will always draw your eyes back. Will Barnes keeps getting better as a vocalist and truly sounds like Brett Michaels, even when he is partaking in some fun banter with the audience. Roger Jamie is lightning in a bottle waiting to be unleashed. And now...there is Mick Hasson. Again, he really only requires one word: Wow!"

As you have likely gathered from the pages of this book, there really is a lot more to putting together a Tribute Band than meets the eye. There is a degree of attention to detail that can separate the haves from the have-nots in this business just as in any other realm. It is my belief that Poison'us has done what needed to be done in order to take that next step and play in bigger venues. The original band has enough depth in the hits department for them to do a full ninety-minute set. Now that they have these two members who are committed to performing a high-energy show, the entire quartet is exponentially better.

I was able to sit down with the original twosome of Will Barnes and Andrew Losli. I dished out the questions, and they have the answers. Since they just underwent a lineup reconstruction, I thought it would be best to lead off with their own road map to finding success in the Tribute Band landscape.

Andrew Losli (Rikki Rockett drums): "You want to look the part, dress the part, and be the part, because you want to give the person that is coming an experience. The memory from high school...or something. And if you're not willing to do the whole thing, you might as well just be a cover band. Sure, some of them (cover bands) might play just one band's material, but if you're not selling the whole thing, it's not gonna be good for the people that come. You might be the best musicians in the world, but if you don't sell it visually…"

Will Barnes (Brett Michaels lead vocals/guitar): "In all honesty, that was the hardest part…dressing up like that part and then trying to be comfortable on stage in that get-up. I've been on stages for thirty years, and to dress up like that, and to go out on that stage (during those first shows), I was just trembling. I thought 'This is so unnatural…I feel like a complete douche-bag.' But in those first rehearsals, I would try to visualize that audience really loving us {laughs} looking like douche-bags. That was the only way I could try and put myself in the moment and pull it off."

Losli: "For me it was the other thing. In the 80's, I had longer hair and stuff, but my parents would have never allowed me to look like that, but I always wanted to look the part and I was happy to go out on stage dressed like that, because I had a license to look like I wanted to when I was fifteen…and I never could. I could walk out there, and there was a reason I was looking like this. I was happy to do it. I love that part of it."

Barnes: "And I always looked the part in the 80's. I had long hair…the super-tight pants and the Spandex. I already did all that. So, to be a grown man and then revert back to dressing like that was like, 'God, I feel ridiculous.' For the longest time, I swear, I wouldn't even let my co-workers know what I did. And when we started making videos I was hoping that nobody found it."

Losli: "The cool thing about our Tribute Band as compared to some is that our costumes are so extreme. So, one day at [venue omitted], they had the line out front waiting to get in. I walked out there and was talking to people in my street clothes. Nobody cared who I was, they didn't even want to talk to me. Later, I went and changed into my costume and then walked out to the people and it was like Mickey Mouse at Disneyland. Everybody wants your attention, strange women wanting to kiss ya {laughs} with their husband sitting right there! It's the weirdest thing. Then, after the show you can take it off and walk out and nobody pays you any attention again."

That was not the first time that I had heard that sort of thing. Mark Thomas and the Appetite for Deception gang recounted similar tales as did many others over the course of the interviews for this book.

Since this band just went through a lineup change, they were the perfect guys to ask in regards to what they look(ed) for in a new member.

Losli: "Somebody who is willing to put on some make-up…dress the part."

Barnes: "They gotta be comfortable in their own skin."

Losli: "You can get a really good guitar player who says they want to do it, and the minute you tell him he's gotta wear a wig, he's okay, but then you say lipstick and they say they can't do that."

Barnes: "And then you get the guitar players that, because of the band we do (Poison), nobody ever gave these guys virtuoso credit. And they never set out to be virtuosos, I've watched the interviews with them. They just wanted to try and write rock-and-roll songs that people would dig. So, a lot of the guitar players that we've had are really skilled guitar players, and they say, 'Oh, this is the easiest stuff in the world.' And then they come in and they actually start to try to play it, and then play it in this get-up. That's when it starts to implode and crumble. I've lost count of how many players we've gone through now...trying to find the guys that are comfortable in this...comfortable in their own skin first off to wear this ridiculous get-up, and then learn this music as it was recorded."

Losli: "And then try to be a showman."

We went through a number of the lineup incarnations and some of the reasons that players did not work out. Again, none of that was important to the book when it comes to who. However, it should be noted that the reasons were mostly boiled down to a lack of commitment by individuals to embrace the roles and give the audience the complete experience.

As with many things that become popular, there are always those who begin to sound the death knell. There is a sentiment that begins to spread that claims the scene is played out or at least on the verge of becoming extinct. I never understood the people who are quick to dismiss something as over simply because they wish it so. Sure, there are always statistics and numbers that can be paraded to show that any point is valid, but being a frequenter of these shows, they only seem to be reaching their apex. I asked Barnes and Losli about the longevity of the Tribute Band scene, what is keeping it alive, and what did they feel was the driving force behind it.

Barnes: "I think that what drives it here is that a precedent has been set. Enough people have seen it and seen the value in it. And that creates that kind of viral effect. Other places could probably create that same effect because everybody's getting old, and everybody wants that time where they can recapture just that hour and fifteen minutes of their youth. They can come to these shows and do that. They know they're not looking at the real band, but they know these guys are making an effort."

Losli: "I do think that the 80's, musically, was very visual. We had MTV. Before that, a lot of people didn't know maybe what the people they were listening to even looked like. They just heard them on the radio. And since MTV stopped, a lot of people once again don't know maybe what Blink-182 looks like. They've heard the music, but they don't know them. Whereas, when I was watching MTV as a kid...it was visual."

Interviewing Poison'us, I had to ask a tough question. Not tough in that it is difficult to come up with an answer, but tough in that I had to risk bruising their egos. And let's face it, we all have one. Nobody likes to be thought or spoken poorly of, but in the world of entertainment, only the naïve think that everybody is on the same playing field. I know many writers far more talented than I will ever be who remain in obscurity. There are also ones that I believe—here would be some of that ego—that are not nearly as good, yet they outsell me in huge numbers. I asked what they believed would take them to the next step.

Barnes: "I think this is one of those things that is definitely demand based. Obviously we've made it a point to not book little tiny rooms that want you to play for just beer. Our first show was in Dante's...several of our shows have been there. The Star Theater. (Both upper end venues when it comes to crowd size.) Our first show was with the Appetite guys. We knew going in that this music, the name...and if we could pull off the look and the stage energy and try to duplicate the sound, that people would dig it. I don't care who you are, or how much you hate Glam Bands or *claim* to hate Glam Bands, somebody likes it...and your girlfriend likes it. I'll play any good gig that comes our way."

Losli: "I used to sit around and try to figure out what can push us further, but I don't anymore. I take it one show at a time now."

Barnes: "Me and Andrew (Losli) are not opposed to alteration. We've done it constantly in this group."

If you are in the local Portland area, I would keep your eyes peeled. This new lineup has taken their game up several notches. They are ready to *Cry Tough*.

19

Looks that Kill

You know that you are getting old when a band that you saw make its debut tour comes through for a massive Farewell Tour. Mötley Crüe is just such a band for me. They are also one of my all-time favorites. They have some deceptively deep lyrics for a metal band and the music just reaches down and hits me deep in my soul.

When I saw Same Ol' Situation for the first time, I was extremely impressed. Jon Abell could be Nikki Sixx's twin. To make things even better, the music was scary-good. I became an instant fan.

A year later, they were booked at a show and I could not wait. Unfortunately, that was the same show that had butchered the sound for Poison'us. This is the not-so-glamorous side of the scene.

"Up next was Same Ol' Situation, a Motley Crüe tribute band that we have seen before and really enjoyed. This set was delayed over thirty minutes while the crew tried to figure out what was keeping the light show from coming on. I do hope it was not the single cable that we could see dangling from the center piece of the lights mounted above the stage. In any case, they NEVER did figure it out. Even better, the sound system actually seemed to get WORSE.

"That did not stop the band from busting their collective asses to try and put on a helluva show. Being in front, at least we could sort of hear the vocals. The feedback loop remained and added a steady low-frequency hum to the ENTIRE set in addition to the vocals being almost impossible to hear.

"By the time Same Ol' Situation wrapped up the set, you could hear the rumblings in the crowd. People were wondering what the hell could be wrong. It had to be fixed by the time the final band took the stage. One of the stage hands was even heard saying that the problem was fixed."

I was able to speak with Abell. There was no need to dredge up bad memories. Instead, we could focus on 2016 being his first time performing at Harefest. That allowed us to talk about what he has done to help put his band in such a good position. Obviously he has some thoughts on what it takes if you want to have a shot at climbing the ladder to Tribute Band success.

Jon Abell (bass): "The whole thing comes down to the authenticity. You want to be as close as you can. We try to do that…especially with the vocals. I mean, anybody can do a guitar or a bass part, but it's the vocals. I think our guy Steve (Rohrbough) does a great job. People like Mark Thomas from Appetite (for Deception) …guys like that. The second thing is that you've gotta look it. And I know that not everybody can do that, but if you put the effort in, you can come across as close. This is something that people are coming to see, and they may not have been able to see this band in their lifetime. So they're coming to see you, and maybe relive that whole thing that they missed. Be true to the music."

The conversation shifted to the degree of support that these bands often show for each other. I asked him what he believed to be the contributing factor the helpful nature that is found from other bands and band members.

Abell: "I think that everybody here wants to see each other succeed and make this bigger and better. It's like a brotherhood. I don't want to say a club, but there really is this brotherhood where everybody comes out to see each other when we can."

If you wonder what sorts of things some of these performers do to prepare for a show, here is your chance.

Abell: "I can only speak for myself, it doesn't matter the size of the show, I treat 'em all as if I were playing at the Rose Garden. (The *original* name of Portland's Moda Center.) People pay to come and see me and they should get the best that I can give. I like to kinda be alone for most of the day until I get to the gig. Which…then the business side has to be dealt with. I like to try and stay calm and relax…and my wife is cool with that. I try to take it easy the night before. Before we go on, I like to have about twenty minutes to myself where I can focus on what's going on and where things are happening."

If you ever find yourself standing across the room from Abell in an audition and want to have a shot at making it in his band should he ever be in need…here are some tips.

Abell: "You're gonna have to do your homework. You have to know the songs. If you are a singer, you're gonna have to have the range. It's not necessarily to me about how great you are…especially an instrument player. Obviously you want them to be able to play every note right. But it's being able to work with that person…to be able to get along with them and have them be a team player."

This is one of the bands that will be making some waves in the sea of Tribute Bands...hopefully for years to come. I can't say this often enough, but if you are in the area and see that they are playing...don't miss their act.

TRIBUTE

20

Classics Never Die

If you are old enough to remember the days of *Midnight Special* and *Don Kirshner's Rock Concert*, then you saw the genesis of music television. These shows featured acts that are now part of the Classic Rock genre. I guess I should be more specific since I heard Def Leppard on a station the other day that bills itself as 'Your Classic Rock Connection!' in its tagline.

When I say Classic Rock, I am talking The Stones, Led Zeppelin, The Who and groups of that era. Much like the 90's music scene, bands from that Classic Rock era did not rely on fancy clothes and such. That is not to say that they did not have an identifiable look…Jagger's lips, his strutting. Keith Richards with his dangling cigarette and attitude. Pete Townsend and that windmill guitar strum. These were all signatures. Yet, it really was all about the music back then. It was an identifiable sound.

For musicians to choose acts from that Classic Rock period, they really need to be focused on the sound. Fortunately, we have Rich Ray. He is considered by many of his peers to be the "Golden Voice" of the Tribute Band scene. He is the vocal front man for Ramble On (Led Zeppelin) and Jukebox Heroes (Foreigner).

Ray is surrounded by a bevy of talent in those acts. He has Brandon Cook and Michael Killian (Appetite for Deception) wielding their guitars with Jukebox Heroes, and Steve Adams taking the role of Jimmy Page with Ramble On.

If you are daring enough, then I invite you to settle in as Ray and Adams share their thoughts on what you need to do if you want a better chance at becoming a successful Tribute Band. What I found interesting here was not exactly a different take on things like the blueprint, but just the laid back feel that came from both Ray and Adams. That is not to say I did not pick up on that sort of vibe with other interviews, but there was truly something different and ethereal about these two performers. I guess that is why they do such a stellar job of tackling rock icons like Led Zeppelin.

Steve Adams (guitar): "You have to have some kind of...I wouldn't say a resemblance physically, but you have to bring some attention to your general presentation. Not only to the sound...the sound is primary, but you have to have some kind of, for lack of a better term, rock-and-roll persona. That can be either distilled into charisma or into clothing. Or...if hair is significant in the band, that's kind of an element that is visual. I've seen some (upstart) Tribute Bands where I thought the presentation should have been a little more Vegas-y in a sense. Attention to how you look. You know, if you have a particular metal band performing, you don't want to go on stage in Hawai'ian shirts. Obviously I am using that as an example to exaggerate some ridiculous presentation, but that attention has to be there. The people who go to see Tribute Bands...the demographic...are people who want to, in a sense, re-live the glory days of their own experience attending shows. It's a nostalgic adventure into re-creating that experience for them. Thirty years ago, people would go to see Elvis Tributes and they want to see the guy in the white suit or whatever their favorite version of Elvis is. In a sense...Tribute Bands recreate that. I assume you have the talent base to put together something that sounds good...I hope you would have that perception of your collective group. If there isn't at least some good visual presentation, it won't be as successful as it could be."

Rich Ray (vocals): "I think, obviously doing your best to emulate the energy and the sound of the music as much as possible. If there are people in your band that have some kind of natural look that obviously fits one of the members that you are paying tribute to, then kind of go with that. I prefer to let individual characteristics of people...the real people that make up the band...I think it is important to let that shine through. Some of the Tribute Bands that I've seen that I really thought were cool were people that I could tell their personalities were there and they weren't one hundred percent trying to imitate or completely replicate whatever person in the band that they were paying tribute to. To me it can often seem more forced. I think any good show, it doesn't matter if it is an original band or a Tribute Band or cover band, you want there to be real energy there. If the act of you trying too hard to pretend that you're somebody else makes you look stilted or too scripted...I think that takes some of the natural energy away. I think you concentrate on energy and the feel of the music over your look."

Considering the very different style of music that they cover in their Tribute library, I was eager ask them about the symbiotic Portland vibe.

Ray: "I think I would attribute the positive attitude in the scene here to the fact that many of the performers here have known each other for probably twenty years or more. A lot of these guys went to high school together. I think for the most part there is definitely a strong sense of community in this scene which is why I have been so happy to be a part of it. It's incredibly supportive and nurturing. I've had people from other bands come and totally bail me out. Kevin Hahn (Stone in Love) came and covered me in Maiden Northwest when my voice was blown out from a gig from the week before. One guy who filled when I screwed up and had the wrong dates for a family vacation (laughs). It's just an amazing community to be a part of."

Adams: "I've known a lot of the people in some of the current Tribute Bands before they were in the Tributes. I've worked with Brandon Cook (Appetite for Deception/Jukebox Heroes) for years. I've known Mark Trees (Motorbreath) and was in an original band with him. We were friends...so it's kind of odd to see your peer group do it. We've all been in projects or rubbed elbows in some way with each other before this even came out. There's an established brotherhood and camaraderie already. I don't think it is even perceived that we're in this competitive thing. It goes along with the general maturity of a lot of this, because we've been through that. Maybe if we were in our twenties we might have that more combative attitude, but it's kinda silly now."

I think that all of us would love a time machine trip...maybe just once. If we could go back in time and give ourselves a piece of advice, what would it be? I asked Rich Ray what he might say to his younger self about how to approach his Tribute career.

Ray: "(Laughs) Well, for me, I think the biggest lesson would be knowing when to say 'no' to something. There was a time when I was taking on too many projects and it was interfering with other aspects of my life. Know your limits. And I would say that if you are going to start a Tribute Band, know ahead of time what your goals are...what you really want to focus on with the band and what you want other people to take from it. We decided early with Ramble On that we weren't going to go overboard with the costumes...wigs...anything like that. We thought that the sound we were able to reproduce when we were 'woodshedding' it was going to be our thing. We were going to leave people feeling like, if they closed their eyes, they heard Led Zeppelin. That was really all that mattered to us."

Asking a guitarist how he would build a band from scratch is always an interesting journey. While this book deals with the Tribute Band scene, there are some tips here that are universal. Still, if Steve Adams ever puts out the word that he is building a band, and you want the inside track to make the cut...listen up.

Adams: "Excluding musicality, it would have to be solid experience in the music industry as a performer. You have to have that actor ability and most people who have that experience just knows how to entertain. You don't just stand there on stage unless whoever you are emulating requires you to. You have to, in a sense, bring that. Apart from musicality, you have to move around on stage. You have to entertain and connect with people. That is significant. You have to have a maturity to understand how business works. Nowadays, everyone in a band does have to participate in dealing with the media. You have a certain amount of responsibility promoting gigs via the various social media platforms versus just some scrambled flyer in a coffee shop…there's more to it. Plus, not only the performance, you have to deal with dynamics in the band…how bands really work and communicate with each other. If you've been through the grind, you know that you have to deal with "that" personality, and if you're upset about something, open communications within the band. Don't just quit out of fury. This is really just like any other business. You work out an issue or come to a compromise. A lot of times, in bands, you don't see that level of maturity and calm to deal with an issue that needs to be dealt with. A lot of times guys don't perceive (bands) as a real job, so they perceive it as something they *want* to do on the side where they don't feel they want to put up with the BS. So they just say 'To hell with this!' and walk out. In a business situation, you wouldn't do that…you treat it a little more seriously. That's what I like in a band. Most of my bands, everyone has that attitude. Nobody abuses a substance before we go on…we are doing our job and treat it with more maturity. That needs to be done in this scene."

Sage advice indeed.

21

Thanks, from the guy in the front row.

I could go on, but I decided to turn over the final chapter to another fan. You've heard enough from me. Let's allow somebody else to share what these bands mean to the people who buy the tickets. If you have seen a show here in Portland, chances are, you have bumped into Dwight Balzer.

This is the guy that these bands have been telling you all about. This is the person in the audience that they strive to entertain. Dwight drives over an hour at least to come to these shows. If you get a moment, go to Google Earth and type in Hood River, Oregon. Now, check out the distance between there and Portland. That is the journey this man makes every time he comes to see these bands perform. He seemed like the perfect person to ask what it was about the Tribute Band scene that captured his attention.

***

Dwight Balzer (fan): "What drew me to the Tribute Band scene in the first place was having a friend (Jeff Buehner) who plays in several bands and he invited me to come see them play in Portland. I'd seen him play in The Dalles…I think at our high school reunion. I checked them out and was totally blown away with the level of talent that I witnessed. It was the very first time and I was hooked. Slowly but surely, I met other people in the bands, the crowd…and I started going to other shows. I found that, from band to band, no matter who I saw, there was this level of professionalism and seriousness that I had not expected. Plenty of people have a garage band or a band that they played with in high school…but these are very dedicated musicians that are very devoted to their craft. I appreciate the hard work they go through in practice to hone their skills as musicians. That is what has kept me coming back for close to three years now. Over that time, I've seen a lot of bands, and they all take their work seriously. It's also clear they truly enjoy performing for the fans, allowing the fans to enjoy the music that they remember from when they were younger. Another thing that I really like is how these bands are so approachable by the people. You can go up before or after the concerts and shake their hands. As you get to know them, they might point or wave from up on stage while they are playing…acknowledging that they see you there supporting them. They are truly grateful to their fans for the support."

That led to talking about just what I have mentioned time and again in this book: the accessibility and approachability of these Tribute Bands and how they are often out mingling with the fans before and after the shows.

Balzer: "One of the things that I found to be the most flattering was that, when I went to these venues early on, if I went up to these guys and said what a great job I thought that they did, they were always quick to say thanks and express how much they appreciated the support for coming out, and then they may talk to you for a couple of minutes. Then they move along and talk to other people, but you felt in that moment like you really were appreciated. Over time, after seeing these bands a number of times, now, they come up to *you* and say, 'Hey, good to see ya! How's it going?' rather than you just coming up to them after the concert to say hi. That's the transition of getting to really know a lot of these guys almost like friends and buddies and not just some random fan. It's like they get to know you just as you get to know them. That is one of the really gratifying things. Plus, you start to meet some of the people in the crowds that are regulars, and you increase your circle of friends that way too."

One of the regular themes from the performers that I interviewed was a sense of humbleness and appreciation for being able to do what they love. Not a single one of these people had what you might consider a "Rock Star" attitude. What they miss is just what degree of an impact they have on the audience. Those of us on this side of the stage see these people as true Rock Stars. Like the old saying goes: "Girls want 'em, and guys wanna be 'em." (Naturally you reverse that gender thing for bands like Barracuda.) So, to the performers, let me reveal to you what the average fan sees when they look at you on stage.

Balzer: "I see very serious, dedicated performers who go all out to give the crowd an exciting experience with the music that they play. They, in my view, are Rock Stars in the sense that there are lots of people in the crowd, including myself, that really get amped up and excited to see them perform…knowing that they are going to give their all-out best and you're gonna have a really great time. It's one thing to buy a ticket to one of those events thinking that maybe this will be a good crowd or concert. But it's like a sporting event. You never really know if it's gonna be a good game or a bad game. But after seeing all these guys play enough times, it's so awesome to know that, when you go, you're automatically gonna have a great time…be around great people…and hear great music. They never fail. A lot of these bands I've gone to see repeatedly are part of Jason Fellman's production, where they come every three months or so in the calendar year and you just know you're gonna have a blast. When it's over, you are totally spent. I drive home, usually over and hour to an hour and fifteen minutes away, and I always leave knowing that I just saw an awesome event. When they say that they're not really rock stars, you see it in the people's eyes, and hear it in their screams…they *are* rock stars to all of us. Just watch the girls in the crowd. The fans do see them as rock stars and I think they deserve it."

That statement also revealed something else. Even the people in the audience know and appreciate Jason Fellman of J-Fell Presents. So I asked Dwight to imagine having Fellman come up and ask him who was missing. What band has yet to be represented in this scene? I asked that same question of many of the bands I interviewed and it was overwhelming. Def Leppard led the votes, but the musicians were quick to point out the degree of "piped in" sound that supports the actual Def Leppard. Most of them are against manufactured tracks being played under their performance. They believe the crowd comes to see live music, not something out of a can. Balzer's vote came as no surprise.

Balzer: "The one band that I would truly love to see is Def Leppard…but I've heard from some of the bands I've talked to that they are just so hard to play. But I tell you what, that is one band that I would love to see. It would hit the ball out of the ballpark. After that…I think Loverboy. I've just always liked them and would love to see a good Loverboy Tribute Band."

Besides Def Leppard, some of the acts that I heard tossed around by various performers included Duran Duran (number two vote getter behind Def Leppard), Cheap Trick, and Ratt. Personally, I think that a few talented ladies need to get together and do perhaps a combo Runaways, Joan Jett, and Lita Ford. By combining the acts, you can still pull off the Tribute look, but now you have enough hits to make up a decent set list. Granted, you may be hampered (much in the same way a Cheap Trick Tribute Band would be by only really being able to build enough strong material to be an opener versus a headliner). I also think there is room for a quality Styx Tribute Band. They absolutely have the catalog depth. And isn't that what is touring now? A glorified Styx Tribute Band with maybe one or two of the original members?

I wrapped up my interview with Dwight by just allowing him to offer up any message he might have for these Tribute Bands.

Balzer: "I want them all to know that, from the bottom of my heart, I thank them for what they do. They provide a very important outlet for a lot of people. There are a lot of folks who have tough jobs, tough family lives, or are just so busy in their daily activities that they just want to go out and have a good time…be entertained, and maybe escape for a little while from life's pressures and problems. You (the Tribute Band performers) provide that outlet for thousands of people all over the Northwest. You've made Portland a hotspot nationwide for these top level Tribute Bands. I can't thank you enough, and I'm so proud of all of you in how you've represented Portland...like having Appetite for Deception on AXS-TV as *The World's Best Tribute Band* for Guns N' Roses. Or whether it's Unchained going to Las Vegas and the Hard Rock for St. Patrick's Day. There's Barracuda who come all the way down from Vancouver, Canada...the Tom Petty Tribute Band (Petty Fever) with Frank Murray who is twice named the Tribute Band of the Year by the industry...he's here in Portland. These are all accomplishments that are just beyond amazing. And to have all these high level players that have accomplished so much...being all from Portland or the area, I can't tell them enough how much I appreciate what they do, because they do provide a solid outlet for people and bring a lot of enjoyment to their lives. In these times when things are tough for a lot of people for a lot of different reasons, it is nice to have them performing for us. It's also equally great that the fans are so supportive of these bands as well. And I do have to give kudos to Jason Fellman again for all his hard work in putting so many fantastic shows together in so many different venues under so many different circumstances. His staff and stage handlers...the sponsors who pitch in their financial support, all these people deserve credit for representing Portland so well for all the people."

Dwight would never assume to speak for everybody, but I think it is safe to say that he does capture a lot of the sentiment felt at least in part by a majority of the fans and spectators who come either regularly or even just casually to these events. His words act as a fitting tribute to the bands who pay tribute to the soundtracks of our lives.

Ramble On - Led Zeppelin Tribute

http://rambleonpdx.com/
https://www.facebook.com/rambleonpdx/
@rambleonpdx
Members: Rich Ray~ Vocals -- Steve Adams~ Guitars -- Pat LeFebvre~ Bass, Keys -- Merrill Hale~ Drums

Motorbreath – Metallica Tribute

https://www.facebook.com/motorbreathNW/
@motorbreathNW
Members: KEVIN STALEY - Jaymz - Vocals/Guitar JOE SPENCER - Larz - Drums -- BOB CAPKA - Krk - Lead Guitar -- MARK TREES - Cliff/Jason/Rob – Bass

J-Fell Presents - Promoter

http://www.j-fell.com/
https://www.facebook.com/JFellPresents/
@JFELLPresents
Jason Fellman
Genre: Tributes / Covers / Originals Rock / Dance / Pop / R&B / Metal

Steelhorse – Bon Jovi Tribute

https://www.facebook.com/morejovi/
@morejovi
Members: Mark Thomas - Lead Vocals Brian McGroovy - Lead Guitar Bryan R Harvey - Keyboards Jeff Buehner - Bass Kevin Rankin – Drums

Unchained – Van Halen Tribute

http://www.unchainednw.com/
https://www.facebook.com/UnchainedVHTribute/
@UnchainedVHTribute
Members: Don Evans aka Diamond Donnie Lee. Jim Schmoltz aka Top Jimmy. Harry Bower aka Taz "Mad Man" Anthony. Dirk Boinker aka Dirk Van Nailen

All Fired Up – The Pat Benatar Experience

http://mur-man.wix.com/allfired-up
https://www.facebook.com/BenatarTributeAct/
@BenatarTributeAct
Members: DL Car (Pat Benatar) Ray Roper (Neil Geraldo) Bob McIntosh Curtis Leippi Brenda Kashmir Adam Wawzonek

Shoot to Thrill – an ACDC Tribute

http://www.j-fell.com/ShootToThrill/
https://www.facebook.com/ShootToThrillAnAcdcTribute/
@shootToThrillAnAcdcTribute
Members: Ted Berry (Angus Young) - Lead Guitar, Evan Berry (Brian Johnson/Bon Scott) – Vocals, Maury Brown (Malcolm Young) - Guitar and Vocals, Kevin Rankin (Phil Rudd) - Drums and Vocals, Jeff Krebs (Cliff Williams) - Bass and Vocals

Jukebox Heroes – Foreigner Tribute

https://www.facebook.com/JukeBoxHeroes.ForeignerTribute/
@JukeBoxHeroes.ForeignerTribute
Members: Rich Ray – Vocals, Brandon Cook - Lead Guitar, Michael Killian - Rhythm Guitar, Jon Friendly – Bass, Eric Rabe – Saxophone, Rich Petko – Keyboards, Andrew Greene - Drums

Poison'us – The Worlds Greatest Poison Tribute Band

http://www.poison-us.com/
https://www.facebook.com/TributeBandPDX/
@TributeBandPDX
Members: Will Barnes as...Bret Michaels - Mick Hasson as...C.C. Deville - Roger Jaime as...Bobby Dall - Andrew Losli as...Rikki Rockett

Monkey Wrench – Foo Fighters Tribute

https://www.facebook.com/Monkeywrenchpdx/
@monkeywrenchpdx
Members: Jon Johnson - Guitars / Lead Vox Chris Beltran - Guitars / Back up KC Peters - Bass / Back up Christian Smith - Drums /Back up

Same Ol' Situation – Motley Crue Tribute Band

https://www.facebook.com/Same-Ol-Situation-Motley-Crue-tribute-band-116312241818699
Members: Steve Rohrbough Jon Abell Andrew Green Derrick Reader

Barracuda – The Essential Tribute to the band Heart

https://www.facebook.com/BenatarTributeAct/
https://www.facebook.com/BarracudaHeartTribute/
@BarracudaHeartTribute
Members: D.L. Car ,Brenda Kashmir ,Bob McIntosh, Ray Roper, Adam Wawzonek, Curtis Leippi

Petty Fever – 2013 & 2014 Tribute Band of the Year

http://www.pettyfever.com/
https://www.facebook.com/PettyFever/
@PettyFever
Members: Frank Murray: Lead Vocal and Guitar, Tim Baitus: Guitar, Steve Kuepker: Bass Guitar, Jack Codron Keyboards, Craig Ostbo: Drums

Stone In Love – Journey Tribute Band

http://www.stoneinlove.com/
https://www.facebook.com/journeytribute/
@journeytribute
Members: Kevin Hahn, Davin, Mike Johnson, Dain Ryan, and Jason Fellman

Grand Royale – A Beastie Boys Tribute

http://www.grandroyalemusic.com/
https://www.facebook.com/GrandRoyaleMusic/
@GrandRoyaleMusic
Members: Kirby aka MCAin't, Justin aka Mike Double D, Jason aka MadRock, Chris aka Tony Oakland, Neehar aka Buster Shabazz, Archie aka White Chocalate Thunder, Miles aka F.M.O.B.

Sonic Temple – A Tribute To The Cult

https://www.facebook.com/sonictemplepdx
@sonictemplepdx
Members: Craig Lower (Vox) ,Brian Harrison (gtr), Brian McGrew (gtr),Samuel Zern (drms) , Ryan Ellsworth (bass)

Appetite for Deception – The most authentic Guns n' Roses Tribute ANYWHERE - AKA Worlds Greatest Tribute Band

http://www.appetitefordeception.com/
https://www.facebook.com/Appetite-for-Deception-282803513246/
@Appetite4D
Members: Michael "Izzy" Killian, Brandon "BC Slash" Cook, Andrew "Andrew Sorum" Greene, WWS "Duff McLuvin", and Mark "Axl M" Thomas

And MANY more that we just don't have room to mention. Search your local area for TRIBUTE BANDS near you.

MAY DECEMBER
Publications

**The growing voice in horror
and speculative fiction.**

Find us at www.maydecemberpublications.com
Or
Email us at contact@maydecemberpublications.com

TW Brown is the author of the *Zomblog* series, his horror comedy romp, ***That Ghoul Ava***, and, of course, the ***DEAD*** series. Safely tucked away in the beautiful Pacific Northwest, he moves away from his desk only at the urging of his Border Collie, Aoife. (Pronounced Eye-fa)

He plays a little guitar on the side...just for fun...and makes up any excuse to either go trail hiking or strolling along his favorite place...Cannon Beach. He answers all his emails sent to twbrown.maydecpub_@gmail.com and tries to thank everybody personally when they take the time to leave a review of one of his works.

His blog can be found at:http://twbrown.blogspot.com

The best way to find everything he has out is to start at his Amazon Author Page:

http://www.amazon.com/TW-Brown/e/B00363NQI6

You can follow him on twitter @maydecpub and on Facebook under Todd Brown, Author TW Brown, and also under May December Publications.

www.ingramcontent.com/pod-product-compliance
Lightning Source LLC
Chambersburg PA
CBHW081147040426
42445CB00015B/1792